HOW TO TEACH STUDENTS TO RE___

Retelling is the reader's account, in his own words, of what he h___ ____ __ ____ ___ been read to him.

FYI

- *Paraphrasing* can be written or oral and typically involves students taking *formal* text and rewriting it or telling about it using *informal* language.
- *Summarizing* is taking the main parts of a text and sharing the main ideas and supporting details in their *original form* and *level of discourse*.

RETELLING (GRADES K-1)

STEP 1

Teach students that they will be learning a habit for comprehension called "retelling," which is stating, in your own words, the most important parts of what you've read.

STEP 2

Teach students that in order to retell successfully, they will need to learn to include what happened at the beginning of the text, the middle of the text and the end of the text.

STEP 3

Model for students how to orally retell what happened in a very short piece of text that you have read aloud. As you model, give students this simple frame to support them.

In the beginning of _____, there was an important event. That event was _____. As I continued to read, I saw that _____ happened. This was important because _____. At the end of _____, _____ took place.

STEP 4

After you have modeled the retelling frame in Step 3 at least five times, have students practice retelling a selection as a whole group, filling out the frame from Step 3 as you go.

STEP 5

Once students have practiced retelling and have firmed up their skills, they should be required to orally retell after every first read.

HOW TO TEACH STUDENTS TO RETELL/RECALL

Recalling is the reader's account of what he has read, told in chronological order. In recalling, the speaker focuses heavily on facts, and answers who, what, when, where, why and how.

RECALLING (GRADES 2-12)

STEP 1

Teach students that they will be learning a habit for comprehension called "recalling," which is their account of the facts of what they've read, told in chronological order.

STEP 2

Teach students that, in order to recall successfully, they will need to learn how to take note of the text's most important information: who, what, when, where, why and how.

STEP 3

Model for students how to orally recall what happened in a short piece of text that you have read aloud. Show students how, while reading each paragraph, you jot down 1-2 words about who, what, when, where, why or how next to the paragraph in the margin.

It is important to model for students that while you are taking notes, you are only writing 1-2 words in the margin, not rewriting the whole piece of text.

STEP 4

Now you will model how to orally recall the story, using the notes you've jotted down in the margin.

In the text _____, first the character(s) _____ was/were introduced. The character(s) then _____ and _____. Then _____ took place. Finally, the text ended with _____.

STEP 5

Once students have practiced recalling and have firmed up their skills, they should be required to orally recall after every first read.

HOW TO TEACH STUDENTS TO RETELL/RECALL

GRADES K-2

Grab and Go Retell/Recall Prompts and Questions for Literature

1. Retell/recall what happened in the first part of the text, the middle, and the end of the text.

2. At the beginning/middle/end of the story ___(character)___ ___(tell what he is doing or did)___ .

3. Describe the characters and the setting for the text, ___(title of text)___ .

4. Use the pictures in the text to help you retell/recall the story, giving at least two examples from the text.

5. What is the problem in the story and how is it solved? Give specific examples from the text to support your answer.

6. ___(Character)___ wanted to ___(action)___ , but ___(problem/conflict)___ .

7. Where and when does the story take place? How does the author let you know this?

8. How does the story end? What words does the author use to describe the ending?

9. What key details did you learn from the illustrations? Do they make sense when you think about what you read?

10. What did the characters do first and second in the story?

Grab and Go Retell/Recall Prompts and Questions for Informational Text

1. What is this text mainly about?

2. ___(Title of text)___ is about ___(main idea)___ .

3. According to the text, what are the ___(number)___ stages/phases of ___(topic)___ ?
Example: According to the text, what are the four stages of fertilization?

4. What does the text say about why ___(topic)___ ___(action)___ ?
Example: What does the text say about why volcanoes erupt?

5. Using the graphic organizer retell/recall the process of ___(topic)___ .

6. As you read about how ___(event)___ and ___(event)___ play out, retell/recall how they are connected to one another. How did the author show that to you?

7. The text describes the sequence of steps in ___(topic)___ . In your own words recall those steps.

8. What is/are the reason(s) the author gives for ___(problem)___ ?

9. Draw pictures to explain the author's main points about ___(topic)___ .

10. Retell/recall all that you learned about ___(topic)___ by reading ___(title of text)___ .

HOW TO TEACH STUDENTS TO RETELL/RECALL

GRADES 3-5

Grab and Go Retell/Recall Prompts and Questions for Literature

1. Retell the central message and at least three key details from the text, _____(title of text)_____ .

2. The central message of _____(title of text)_____ is _____(central message)_____ . Three key details are _____(key detail 1)_____ , _____(key detail 2)_____ , and _____(key detail 3)_____ .

3. What is the sequence of events of _____(title of text)_____ ? Use the signal words first, next, and last in your retelling/recalling.

4. In your own words describe the characters and setting. Explain how the author reveals both, using particular examples from the story.

5. What is the plot of the text? Give examples of how the author chose to engage you in the plot throughout the text.

6. Use the key details of the text to retell/recall the central message. Explain how the details you shared from the text support the central message.

7. Describe the solution to the problem in the story. How did the author use the characters' actions to highlight the solution for the reader?

8. The problem in the text was _____(problem)_____ . The problem was solved when _____(name of character[s])_____ _____(action)_____ .

9. Why do you think the author made the decision to title the story _____(title of text)_____ ? Was the title important throughout the narrative? Did it play a role?

10. What is the lesson in _____(title of text)_____ and how does it relate to common themes that we've encountered in other text?

Grab and Go Retell/Recall Prompts and Questions for Informational Text

1. Retell/recall the problem or issue described in the text and the solutions the author suggested.

2. Prior to reading the whole text, determine what inferences you can make about _____(topic)_____ ? List three pieces of information from the text that can help you make those inferences.

3. What key details describe the main idea of the text? Give several examples of details that were included, but did not have bearing on the main idea.

4. What causes _____(topic)_____ to _____(effect)_____ ? *Example: What causes dormant volcanoes to erupt?*

5. What do you know now about _____(topic)_____ ? If you were going to give someone the gist of what you've learned in two sentences, what would you say?

6. Use the key details presented in _____(title of text)_____ to summarize _____(topic)_____ .

7. Who were the key figures during the _____(event)_____ ? How did their involvement impact the event?

8. What happens when _____(scientific process)_____ ? *Example: What happens when bears hibernate?*

9. In your notes, why did you highlight these particular ideas and not others?

10. Did the author follow a linear path in telling you the facts about _____(topic)_____ ? How did the structure of the text help you recall the most important information?

HOW TO TEACH STUDENTS TO RETELL/RECALL

GRADES 6-8

Grab and Go Retell/Recall Prompts and Questions for Literature

1. _____(Word 1)_____ and _____(word 2)_____ are the two most important words that help me get the gist of the paragraph.

2. While reading _____(title of text)_____, these three events _____(event 1)_____, _____(event 2)_____, and _____(event 3)_____ helped me understand the moral of the story.

3. I now have a better understanding of the main character because _____(character's actions)_____.

4. The key details of this chapter in chronological order are _____(detail 1)_____, _____(detail 2)_____, and _____(detail 3)_____.

5. The orientation of this piece of text is _____(who)_____, _____(what)_____, _____(when)_____, _____(where)_____, _____(why)_____ and _____(how)_____.

6. In the beginning, _____(event 1)_____. Next, _____(event 2)_____. Then, _____(event 3)_____. Finally, _____(event 4)_____.

7. The big ideas presented at the beginning of the text are _____(idea 1)_____, _____(idea 2)_____, and _____(idea 3)_____.

8. The new information presented later in the text is _____(new information)_____. Its meaning to the whole story is important because _____(reason 1)_____, _____(reason 2)_____, _____(reason 3)_____.

9. Provide explanations for the motivations behind the main character's actions.

10. I used my inferencing skills as I read to determine _____(details)_____ about the characters and their changes throughout the text. I believe the author chose to not directly state this because _____(reason 1)_____, _____(reason 2)_____.

Grab and Go Retell/Recall Prompts and Questions for Informational Text

1. This section of the article is mostly about _____(main idea)_____.

2. The first chunk of text I read was about _____(main idea 1)_____. The second chunk of text was about _____(main idea 2)_____. The last chunk of text was about _____(main idea 3)_____.

3. The key details of this chapter in chronological order are _____(detail 1)_____, _____(detail 2)_____, and _____(detail 3)_____.

4. What are two words from each paragraph that can explain the gist of this section?

5. Identify and recall the sequence of events from the article.

6. Identify and recall what caused particular actions/events and their effects.

7. Identify the key details that support the central idea of the article.

8. How does identifying key details help lead you to the main idea?

9. Now that you have read the text once, what clues did the author give that he wanted to inform/persuade/entertain the reader with this text?

10. The author uses the terms _____(word 1)_____ and _____(word 2)_____ to describe the solution near the end of the text. Why were those terms so important, do you think?

HOW TO TEACH STUDENTS TO RETELL/RECALL

GRADES 9-12

Grab and Go Retell/Recall Prompts and Questions for Literature

1. In this story/play/poem, the following happens: _(summarize the events)_ . The key ideas introduced by the author were _(idea 1)_ , _(idea 2)_ and _(idea 3)_ . _(Idea 1)_ is included because _(tell why it matters)_ . _(Idea 2)_ is included because _(tell why it matters)_ . _(Idea 3)_ is included because _(tell why it matters)_ .

2. Which specific details from the text are important to mention about _(event)_ ? What does the author say about this idea over the course of the text?

3. The setting of this story is _(time, place and atmosphere)_ . Use specifics from the text as you recall.

4. The character, _(character)_ , is involved in _(situation/problem)_ and he _(tell what he says, does, thinks and feels)_ .

5. The most important and complex character is _(character)_ . He is important because he contributes to the text by _(give textual evidence of why he is important and complex)_ . Tell how you know this and why this is important to the text.

6. What genre is this piece of literature?

7. Why do you believe the author gives vague details about _(event)_ as it happens, requiring you to infer?

8. Is there a certain part of the text that the author leaves undone or incomplete? Give specific examples of how the author chooses to leave out information and your thoughts on why.

9. Recall the most interesting interactions between the two pivotal characters in the text. How does the author use specific instances or scenes to highlight these interactions?

10. Using specific details and scenarios from the text, tell how the main character developed over the course of the story.

Grab and Go Retell/Recall Prompts and Questions for Informational Text

1. This text contains the following key ideas about _(topic)_ : _(key idea 1)_ and _(key idea 2)_ .

2. This text emphasizes the following conclusions: _(conclusions and how the text highlights them)_ .

3. How precise, accurate and detailed is the evidence drawn from the text? How do these events and ideas interact with each other to shape the meaning of _(main topic)_ ?

4. The _(process, phenomenon, or idea)_ evolves over the course of the text by _(details)_ .

5. The ideas and facts presented in the text change in _(describe in terms of their meaning, importance, or effect over the course of the text)_ .

6. The central idea of the text is _(central idea)_ . The author brings the central idea to light by highlighting these supporting details: _(supporting detail 1)_ , _(supporting detail 2)_ and _(supporting detail 3)_ .

7. As you look at the order in which the author rolled out the points in this text, what connections about the importance of the order can you make?

8. Look at how the author analyzes the multiple points on _(topic)_ . Identify and describe his bias, if any.

9. The text gives the following key distinctions or inconsistencies: _(key distinctions or inconsistencies)_ .

10. Which specific details are most important to cite? How are these elements connected by the author through categories, stages or other elements?

HOW TO TEACH STUDENTS TO SUMMARIZE

*To **summarize** is to construct a brief statement about the main parts of a text so that the reader can quickly digest the most important information.*

A SIMPLE SUMMARY INCLUDES THE FOLLOWING

✓ **One opening statement that outlines the gist of the text**

✓ **One to two statements about the big ideas from the text**

Literature

For literature or narrative text include a statement about:

√ The setting
√ The main character described in one adjective
√ The climax
√ The resolution

Informational Text

For informational text include a statement about:

√ The purpose of the text
√ The central idea
√ The structure of the text
√ Two supporting points

✓ **A concluding restatement of the gist of the text**

HOW TO TEACH STUDENTS TO SUMMARIZE

SUMMARIZE

	LITERATURE	INFORMATIONAL TEXT
STEP 1	Teach and model how to scan text and highlight three adjectives or phrases describing the setting.	Teach and model how to look at headings, sub-headings, italicized words, bolded words, pictures, diagrams, labels and captions to see what hints these give about the central idea.
STEP 2	Teach and model how to scan text and highlight three adjectives or phrases describing the main character(s) of the text.	Teach and model how to determine the purpose of/for the text. Did the author write to entertain, persuade, provide an opinion, compare and contrast two things or inform you about a topic?
STEP 3	Teach and model how to scan text and highlight several words or phrases describing three important events in the text.	Teach and model how to look at the structure of the text and how the text is organized. Is it chronological, flashback, multiple perspectives or in order of importance?
STEP 4	Teach and model how to scan text and highlight several words or phrases describing the climax of the text.	Teach and model how to condense notes from Steps 1-3 and produce a statement about the central idea of the text.
STEP 5	Teach and model how to cross out unimportant or unnecessary information.	Teach and model how to determine the two to three most important points in support of the central idea.
STEP 6	Teach and model how to refine notes to include key terms and vocabulary from the text.	Teach and model how to refine notes to include key terms and vocabulary from the text.
STEP 7	Teach and model how to use the notes from Steps 1-6 to create a Simple Summary (refer to "A Simple Summary" from the front of this tab).	Teach and model how to use the notes from Steps 1-6 to create a Simple Summary (refer to "A Simple Summary" from the front of this tab).
STEP 8	Teach and model how to determine whether a summary is objective by asking these questions: • Have I used ideas and terms directly from the text? • Could someone who had not read the text previously have the gist of it following my summary?	Teach and model how to determine whether a summary is objective by asking these questions: • Have I used ideas and terms directly from the text? • Could someone who had not read the text previously get the gist of it from my summary?

HOW TO TEACH STUDENTS TO SUMMARIZE

GRADES K-2

If students struggle to find the central idea, then:	If students struggle to determine supporting details, then:	If students struggle to determine what relevant details are, then:
• Use text with pictures and ask the students to determine what the text will be about by only looking at the pictures. Then read the text to/with the students and discuss if their ideas based on the pictures were accurate. • Prompt students to use picture cards that match the text. This will help students to identify the characters, setting, and events in a story. • Use a visual story map and together identify the "who", "where", "when" details and key events of the story. Students can then practice summarizing by using the story map.	• Model for students how to listen carefully to a question about the text and find the answer directly in the text. • During a first read, model for students how you circle the main idea of the text. Then use a highlighter to highlight two or three specific details that support the main idea. • Teach students to ask themselves, "What information helps me understand the main idea even more?"	• Write the topic of an informational text or the title of the narrative text above a T-Chart. Write "important detail" on one side and "unimportant detail" on the other side of the chart. Have students share details from the text and as a class decide if the detail is important or unimportant. Ensure that students can explain why, then provide correction and affirmation. • Model for students how the details under "important" can be combined into a summary statement. • Teach students this frame: In ___(name of text)___, ___(supporting detail 1)___, ___(supporting detail 2)___, and ___(supporting detail 3)___ are all important details that help me to understand ___(name the topic/description)___ of the theme more.

HOW TO TEACH STUDENTS TO SUMMARIZE

GRADES 3-5

If students struggle to find the central idea, then:

- Preview the text or teach pronunciation and meaning of critical vocabulary words to build necessary background knowledge and provide context.

- Model how to look for headings and subheadings in informational text and to identify characters, setting, and events in literary text to determine the central idea.

- Teach students this frame: The headings and subheadings for this text are ___(heading)___, ___(subheading)___, ___(subheading)___ therefore the central idea is likely ___(central idea)___.

If students struggle to determine supporting details, then:

- Choose an advertisement. Use the product as the main idea, and teach how to select several features of the product as supporting details.

- Teach students key words that often clue the reader into supporting details such as: *one*, *another*, *finally*.

- Teach students this frame: Three supporting details from the text, ___(title of text)___, are ___(detail 1)___, ___(detail 2)___, and ___(detail 3)___. These three details support the central idea ___(central idea)___.

If students struggle to determine what relevant details are, then:

- Have students create lists of facts from the text. Working with a partner, have students order the facts from "most connected to the main idea" to "least connected to the main idea." Then have students write a summary sentence using the most connected ideas.

- Teach students to ask, "Does ___(detail)___ tell precisely about ___(topic)___?"

- Work with a text that has several irrelevant details and cross out the irrelevant details, then reread the text that remains.

HOW TO TEACH STUDENTS TO SUMMARIZE

GRADES 6-8

If students struggle to find the central idea, then:

- Teach students to examine the title of a text and consider how the title gives clues about the central idea.

- Ask students to choose 3-5 words that are important to the text and create a summary statement based on those words.

- Teach students to cross-out the information in the text that is not likely the central idea.

If students struggle to determine supporting details, then:

- Model for students how to sort essential and non-essential information: *"Students, I would like you to underline the claim in this article: it's in the first paragraph, second sentence. Now, I would like for you to highlight any detail in this article that supports our known claim. Next, with your partner, share your highlighted text, and in one sentence justify why the details you highlighted support the claim."*

- Ask students to use this sentence frame to determine the relationship between claim and supporting details:
  If ___(supporting detail)___,
  then ___(claim)___.
  For example: If forty-five percent of the work force is below the poverty line, then the minimum wage must be raised.

- Teach students to ask a series of questions: *Did the details help me understand the central idea? Do the supporting details have a more narrow focus than the central idea? Did the details lead me in the same line of thinking as the central idea or did they take me in another direction?*

If students struggle to determine what relevant details are, then:

- Ask students to rank the details' relevance on a continuum of 1 to 10 and justify their ranking.

- Ask students to take out the ideas that they think are least important, and then rank the other details in order of priority to support their central idea.

- Ask students to create a circle on a piece of paper. Students will cut the copy of the paragraph apart by sentence. Next, have students physically place the sentences from the paragraph that connect to the central claim in the middle of the circle and the irrelevant sentences will be placed on the outside of the circle. Have students give evidence to support their decisions.

HOW TO TEACH STUDENTS TO SUMMARIZE

GRADES 9-12

If students struggle to find the central idea, then:	If students struggle to determine supporting details, then:	If students struggle to determine what relevant details are, then:
• Show students how to scan the introduction and the conclusion, as the author typically shares the central idea in one or both places in the text. • Model for students how to scan the text and list all possible central ideas, then determine which idea is most developed in the text. • Teach students to highlight in one color all of the similar ideas/trends throughout the text. For each different line of thinking or trend, use a different highlighter. Ask students which of the ideas/trends are most supported (have the most highlights) and lead them to the conclusion that is likely the central idea of the text.	• Ask students to identify the cause and effect relationships. • Ask students to recognize sequence or time-order words. • Ask students to look for information provided by the author to back up their claims such as examples, details or quotations.	• Encourage students to code the text with underlines, labels or numbers on all the words, images or other details related to the central idea, then determine how these evolve throughout the text. • Demonstrate/model how to trace the development of ideas throughout the text. • Ask students what details (facts, events or relationships) are so integral to the text that they must be included in the summary.

HOW TO TEACH TEXT STRUCTURE

Text structure is the way a text is organized and refers to the different forms the author uses to build the text. Examples of text structure are: description, sequence, problem & solution, cause & effect and compare & contrast.

TEXT STRUCTURE CLUE WORDS

DESCRIPTION

- to illustrate
- is a feature of
- for instance
- such as

SEQUENCE

- before
- following
- meanwhile
- then

PROBLEM & SOLUTION

- because
- therefore
- this led to
- thus

CAUSE & EFFECT

- as a result of
- the effect of
- is caused by
- so that

COMPARE & CONTRAST

- compared with
- otherwise
- yet
- instead of

HOW TO TEACH TEXT STRUCTURE

	ACTION STEPS	SAMPLE SCRIPT
STEP 1	Teach what text structure is	*"Ladies and gentlemen, today I'm going to begin teaching you a very important trick that will help you better understand what you are reading. This trick is called 'understanding text structure' and we will be working in the upcoming weeks to master this skill.* *Text structure is the way the author chooses to organize the text. For example, when we read our Science book yesterday, particularly on p. 39, the author gave us step-by-step directions. These step-by-step directions gave us a clue that the author organized his text using 'sequence' as his text structure."*
STEP 2	Teach one text structure at a time, starting with the most common (description) and then work through the other structures	*"Today, I'm going to teach our first text structure and the one that is most common: description. The description text structure is organized like an outline with major ideas at the beginning and more detail as you continue reading."*
STEP 3	Teach students how they should use clues to determine the text structure during a first read.	*"Okay, I'm going to take this new piece of text and model for you how I dig in and pay attention to the organization and the words within the text. This will help me clue in to the type of structure.* *Some key words that I need to look for that give me clues that I am reading a descriptive piece are: to illustrate, is a feature of, for instance, and such as. When I see these kinds of words, this gives me a clue about the structure. Let me show you that now."* Model with grade level text how you use the key words to identify the author's choice of text structure.
STEP 4	Teach students how text structure can improve their comprehension	*"One thing that we must think about is how text structure helps us understand and comprehend what we read. When I know the structure of the text, it helps me focus on important concepts and relationships, predict what's to come, and monitor my comprehension while I read.* *We know that when we pay close attention to the text and how it's structured, we organize the ideas and thoughts about the text more efficiently in our minds. Text structure is a tool for improving comprehension."*
STEP 5	When students are engaging in a first or second read of a text, ask text structure specific questions	*"The author chose to use the descriptive text structure to share information on the Holocaust. How would your understanding of the topic and events have changed if a different text structure had been used?"* *"The author uses time/order words to describe the events of November 14th in the narrative. Without those time/order words, how might the reader get confused or overwhelmed with details?"*
STEP 6	Repeat Steps 1-5 with sequence, problem & solution, cause & effect, compare & contrast	

How to Teach Students to Critically Think About Text

HOW TO TEACH TEXT STRUCTURE

GRADES K-2

Text Structure Models and Think-Alouds

Description

Text written using the descriptive text structure can help readers understand a topic better. For example, this text is about the Crow Indian Fair in Montana. Hmm, I don't know much about the Crow tribe and I think this fair might be different than fairs that I'm used to. Listen as I read a few sentences:

> The Crow Indian Fair is held at the end of every summer, usually in August, for several days. Many people come from all around to take part in or just to watch all the dancing and to hear the drums. There are many vendors selling their wares of jewelry mostly made of brightly colored beads and adorned with feathers.

Well, I can certainly imagine some sights and sounds at the Crow Indian Fair and the descriptive details the author writes helps me to understand the topic better.

Which text structure helps readers create pictures in their minds about a topic?

Sequence

When a text is structured in a sequence, or order, it helps a reader comprehend the steps or process better. For example, if I read a text about how to create an app it would be most helpful if the steps for creating one were in sequence that tells the first step, the second step, the next step, and the last step. If all the steps were jumbled and out of sequence it would be hard to comprehend and make it very difficult to follow along and create an app.

Which text structure do authors use to show the order of events?

Problem/Solution

When an author wants to show how a problem is solved he will use the text structure of problem and solution. Follow along as I read this text.

> Many countries, including the United States, have a problem: many of their citizens are homeless. They have no permanent place to sleep and often go without regular meals. An international humanitarian group is providing some solutions. They are organizing groups of people to fix up abandoned buildings for the homeless to sleep in and preparing healthy, warm meals.

So the problem was clearly stated by the author in this text in the first sentence (read the first sentence). The author used the signal word "problem," (circle the word, "problem"). The author shares one solution to the problem and even uses the word solution in the sentence right before stating the solution (read the sentence and circle the word, "solution").

Which text structure do authors use to show how a problem is solved?

Cause & Effect

When an author wants to explain how one event causes another to happen he could use the text structure of cause and effect. Follow along in your text as I read.

> Snowmen only last while it's cold outside. As soon as the weather warms up enough it causes the snow to melt and, as a result, the snowman becomes a blob of slushy snow.

Aha! I read some clue words that help me to understand that the author is using the cause and effect text structure. In the text I just read, (read the word "causes" and the phrase "as a result") I can tell that the effect of the weather warming up is the snowman melts into a blob of slushy snow.

Which text structure do authors use to explain how one event or action causes something else to happen?

Compare & Contrast

Let's use this text about cars to better understand the text structure of compare and contrast. Authors use compare and contrast to help readers comprehend how two or more people, places or things are alike or how they're different. Listen.

> The two cars are very different. Both cars can be driven and both are painted bright colors. One is small with extra-large smooth tires and has numbers painted on the hood and doors. However, the other car is bigger and is painted all in one color with no numbers.

Okay, the clue word "both" tells me I'm going to learn how the cars are alike and the clue word "however" signals to me that I'm going to learn how the cars are different.

Which text structure do authors use to explain how things are alike and how they are different?

HOW TO TEACH TEXT STRUCTURE

GRADES 3-5

Text Structure-Specific Questions for Informational Text

1. Some characteristics of ___(topic)___ are ___(characteristic 1)___ , ___(characteristic 2)___ and ___(characteristic 3)___ . *Example: Some characteristics of elephants are they are very large mammals, their sounds can travel several miles and they can live in multiple regions in Africa.*

2. How does the text describe the ___(topic)___ ?

3. What are three characteristics of ___(topic)___ ?

4. The process of ___(process)___ is sequenced in this order. First, ___(stage 1)___ , next, ___(stage 2)___ , last, ___(stage 3)___ . *Example: The process of meeting the U.S. Constitution's requirements to be able to be a Presidential candidate is sequenced in this order: first, a person must be a natural born citizen, next, a person must be at least thirty-five years old, and lastly must have been a U.S. resident for at least fourteen years.*

5. Based on the text what is the sequence for ___(process)___ ?

6. After the first step in ___(process)___ , what is the next step?

7. One solution to ___(problem)___ is to ___(solution)___ .

8. Who or what does the author claim is part of the problem?

9. The text, ___(title of text)___ , shows cause and effect. The cause is ___(cause)___ and the effect is ___(effect)___ .

10. What signal words in this text show that the text structure is cause and effect?

11. In, ___(title of text)___ , I read that ___(topic 1)___ and ___(topic 2)___ are similar because ___(describe how they are similar)___ . They are also different because ___(describe how they are different)___ .

12. The author used the structure of compare and contrast to write ___(title of text)___ . How does this structure help the reader to understand the characters better?

Text Structure-Specific Questions for Literature

1. The author, ___(author)___ describes the character ___(character)___ as ___(description of character)___ .

2. Why might the author have written such thorough descriptions of the characters in this text?

3. First in the text, ___(title of text)___ , ___(event 1)___ . Later, ___(event 2)___ . In the end, ___(event 3)___ .

4. The structure of this text is sequence which provides the steps or order of something. What are the sequence of events in this text?

5. What are the signal words the author uses that shows the reader that the text structure of ___(text structure)___ was used to organize this text?

6. ___(Character)___ had a problem. The problem was ___(problem)___ . This led to ___(event)___ .

7. Was the solution the character came up with a good solution to the problem? Why or why not?

8. As a result of ___(cause)___ ___(effect)___ .

9. What caused ___(character)___ to ___(effect)___ in the story ___(title of text)___ ?

10. ___(Character 1)___ and ___(character 2)___ are alike because ___(describe how they are alike)___ . However, they are different because ___(describe how they are different)___ . *Example: Henry and Julie are alike because they both end up in the principal's office for breaking many school rules. However, they are different because Henry breaks rules when he wants attention from the principal and Julie breaks rules when she wants to get sent home to play with her animals.*

11. How does the author compare the two characters in the text?

12. How does the setting in this text compare to the setting in ___(title of second text)___ ?

HOW TO TEACH TEXT STRUCTURE

GRADES 6-8

Text Structure-Specific Questions for Informational Text

1. Identify four characteristics of this text that prove the text's structure is ___(text structure)___.
2. How does the text make distinctions between ___(topic 1)___ and ___(topic 2)___?
3. The text's central idea is ___(central idea)___, I know this because ___(example 1)___, ___(example 2)___, and ___(example 3)___.
4. Does the central idea span over time? How do you know? Explain your thinking.
5. The problem in the text was ___(problem)___. The author reveals the solution in ___(sentence/paragraph/chapter)___.
6. Explain why the author chose the problem/solution text structure to contribute to the overall meaning of the text?
7. The problem in the text was ___(problem)___. The solution in the text was ___(solution)___. I would have chosen ___(student's own solution)___.
8. Determine two effects from the ___(title)___, and describe their impact on the central idea.
9. According to ___(title of text)___, the effects of ___(action)___, caused ___(effect 1)___, ___(effect 2)___ and ___(effect 3)___.
10. What characteristics of text structure in ___(title 1)___ compare with ___(title 2)___? Explain your thinking.
11. Compare the text structure of ___(text 1)___ and ___(text 2)___ and describe in a paragraph how they contribute to the overall meaning of the text.
12. The topics compared are ___(topic 1)___ and ___(topic 2)___. The similarities are ___(similarity 1)___, ___(similarity 2)___ and ___(similarity 3)___.

Text Structure-Specific Questions for Literature

1. How does the text structure the author chose contribute to the narrative? Use examples from the text in your analysis.
2. The author uses a combination of structures. The structures are ___(structure 1)___ and ___(structure 2)___. The clue words that helped me decide the type of structure are ___(word 1)___, ___(word 2)___ and ___(word 3)___.
3. How does the manipulation of time contribute to the narrative? Use examples from the text in your analysis.
4. Why does the author change the time frame in paragraph ___(#)___?
5. Which sentence from the selection explains the character's primary conflict?
6. Analyze the ___(section of the text)___ to determine when and where the author alludes to the problem in the text.
7. Look at paragraph ___(#)___. Which sentence makes the biggest impact on the solution in the narrative?
8. In ___(name of text)___ the author reveals the ___(conflict)___ in the novel first by ___(description of event)___. The reason for the author doing this is ___(explain your thinking)___.
9. How would the meaning change if we took out the ___(stanza/chapter/scene)___?
10. Analyze ___(text 1)___ and ___(text 2)___, and explain the differences in how the authors used text structure to build the rising action in the story.

HOW TO TEACH TEXT STRUCTURE

GRADES 9-12

Text Structure-Specific Questions for Informational Text

1. From the author's description of ___(central idea)___, we can infer that ___(inference)___.

2. The author uses a series of ___(explain wording/paragraph structures)___ to gain the reader's attention. What effect does this style choice have on the reader?

3. What key points does the writer attempt to emphasize and in what order?

4. The ___(central idea)___ is organized in the text by the following events: ___(event 1)___, ___(event 2)___ and ___(event 3)___.

5. Although ___(problem)___ is a problem, there are also some possible solutions. One solution is ___(possible solution)___. An alternative is ___(alternative solution)___. For each main point, discuss specific examples that further explain the solutions.

6. Due to ___(cause)___, I expect that ___(results)___.

7. According to the article, all of the statements below are reasons why ___(comparison)___ except ___(contrast)___.

8. The writer of this piece chose to show ___(event)___ rather than ___(another event)___. Why do you think the writer made this choice?

9. The video clip, newspaper article and diary entry had ___(commonalities)___. What elements were included in each that contradicted the other?

Text Structure-Specific Questions for Literature

1. How does the author introduce characters and develop them in the story? ___(Character)___ is introduced in the ___(location in text)___ during ___(event)___.

2. Which of the author's decisions most impacts the elements of the story and how they develop or connect over time?

3. Explain how a given event relates to prior events. Explain why the order is important.

4. How did ___(character)___ try to solve the problem? Did his solution work? How did ___(character)___'s solution impact other characters in the story?

5. Write a scene that might have occurred if ___(certain event happened)___.

6. Which conclusions might leave the reader ___(confused, sad, angry, reassured, etc.)___? Explain with evidence from the text.

7. The ___(cause)___ was experienced by ___(character 1)___, ___(character 2)___, ___(character 3)___. What were the results of each of the characters' actions?

8. The analogy, ___(analogy)___, helps the reader understand the comparison between ___(two or more things being compared)___.

9. How does each author view an important historical/cultural issue differently or in the same way? *Example: Societal crime and guilt in The Scarlet Letter vs. Crime and Punishment.*

10. How does a specific literary movement influence each work? *Example: Modernism in Hemingway and F. Scott Fitzgerald, Transcendentalism in Thoreau and Emerson.*

HOW TO TEACH THEME

Theme is the lesson or message of the text that is typically a view of life, human nature or elements of society.

THE MOST COMMON THEMES IN LITERATURE

Man Struggles Against Nature

Man is always at battle with human nature, human tendencies or the aging process

Man Struggles Against Societal Pressure

Mankind is always struggling to determine if society's way is the best way for him to live

Man Struggles to Understand Divinity

Mankind tries to understand and make peace with God

Crime Does Not Pay

Honesty is valued and criminals will eventually be caught

Overcoming Adversity

Man accepts a challenging situation and turns it into triumph

Friendship is Dependent on Sacrifice

You must be willing to occasionally set aside your own desires for the benefit of the friendship

The Importance of Family

It is honorable to make sacrifices for family in order to overcome life's adversities

Yin and Yang

Just when you think life is finally going to go your way, something challenging happens to balance it all out

Love is the Worthiest of Pursuits

Love conquers all

Death is Part of the Life Cycle

Death and life are intricately connected

Sacrifices Bring Reward

Sacrifices and hard work pay off in the end and are worth the challenges endured along the way

Human Beings All Have the Same Needs

Rich or poor, educated or not, all human beings want to have their basic needs met

THEME

HOW TO TEACH THEME

STEP 1

Using three adjectives and specifics from the text, describe the character at the beginning.

At the beginning of the text the character was _____, _____ and _____.

STEP 2

Using three adjectives and specifics from the text, describe the character at the end.

At the end of the text the character had changed to _____, _____ and _____.

STEP 3

In two sentences or less, describe the event that caused the character to change.

The climax or turning point in the text was _____.

This event caused the character to change from _____ to _____ because _____.

STEP 4

In light of your sentences from Step 3, make a decision about which of the Common Themes best describes the text (refer to "Common Themes" from the front of this tab).

If there are more than two themes that fit, use evidence from the text to make the best choice.

STEP 5

Share or write about the theme using this frame:

"The theme became apparent as I analyzed the character and found _____.

When I compared and contrasted the character from beginning to end in relation to the climax of the text, I found that the character had changed from _____ to _____.

I concluded that the theme of the text is _____."

THEME

HOW TO TEACH THEME

GRADES K-2

Grab and Go Theme Prompts and Questions for Informational Text

1. In this text, _____(title of text)_____, I can predict by reading the title, viewing the illustrations or charts, and looking at the headings that the main topic of this text is probably _____(main topic)_____. This will help me begin to figure out the theme of the text.

2. As I read about _____(main topic)_____ in the text _____(title of text)_____, I learned that _____(key detail 1)_____ by reading that _____(quote from text)_____. The next key detail _____(key detail 2)_____ is found _____(quote from text)_____. The last key detail _____(key detail 3)_____ is found _____(quote from text)_____.

3. I predicted that the main topic of the text was _____(main topic)_____. This prediction is supported by the key details in the text and is what the text is mainly about.

4. This informational text is about _____(main topic)_____ and is supported in the text by these key details: _____(key details found in the text)_____. This information helps me understand the theme of the text.

5. Once you have read the text, what is one lesson or one piece of advice that you have learned?

Grab and Go Theme Prompts and Questions When Using Two Sources

1. When I compare the two texts, I find some similarities, or key details that are the same. They are _____(key details that are the same for both texts)_____.

2. I also find some key details that are contrasting or different when I analyze the two texts. The key details that are different are _____(key details that are different)_____.

3. The two texts about _____(main/central idea or topic)_____ have similarities and differences. First, they are similar because both texts _____(how the texts are the same)_____. On the other hand, the texts differ because _____(how the texts differ)_____. Therefore, by comparing and contrasting these two texts I can see how some key details are the same and some key details are different.

4. Do you think that the authors of the two sources agree with one another? What information in the text supports your ideas?

5. Let's look at two different pieces of text with the same theme. What ideas, actions or facts could be taken from one piece of text to support the theme of the other?

Sample Assessment Questions - Theme

- Listen to two passages about _____(topic)_____. Click on the pictures that represent similar ideas in both passages.

- After listening to the passage, select the picture that identifies the main topic. Below that picture, draw three key details that _____(support the main topic)_____.

- Read the two passages. What is the main topic of the two texts? Read the statements below and place each statement into the box labeled 'similar' or into the box labeled 'different' to show the comparison of the two texts.

HOW TO TEACH THEME

GRADES 3-5

Grab and Go Theme Prompts and Questions for Informational Text

1. What reasons does the author of the text give to help drive home his message or theme? Which of the reasons are stronger and why? Which are weaker, in your opinion?

2. Does the structure of the text and how it is organized give you hints about the author's main theme or message? How so?

3. Before I read the text, _(title of text)_ , I thought _(idea 1)_ , _(idea 2)_ and _(idea 3)_ about the topic. Now that I understand the author's message and the theme of the text, I now think _(idea)_ .

4. If the author had started the writing process with one guiding message or theme statement, what do you think that would have been?

5. Informational text is organized differently from literature, as we know, but some of the same emotions about the text can be felt while reading. Did the author use emotion or evoke feelings in you that helped drive his message or theme home?

Grab and Go Theme Prompts and Questions When Using Two Sources

1. How did the two authors use similar tone and language to drive home the theme of _(theme)_ ?

2. When you analyze this _(text 1)_ and this _(text 2)_ , you realize that they have the same theme: _(theme)_ . How did the authors take two, very different forms of literature and produce the same theme?

3. When we read these two different accounts of _(topic)_ , we realize that the authors use the same facts to drive home different themes or lessons. Describe the similarities and differences in the authors' wording, text structure and tone.

4. The two authors, _(author 1)_ and _(author 2)_ , both use a different series of events to help the reader understand the basic theme of _(theme)_ . Describe how _(author 1)_ developed the series of events in the text and how _(author 2)_ developed the series of events.

5. The author _(author)_ wrote two selections on the same topic, but with very different themes or messages. Analyze the two pieces of literature and determine which of his two themes you believe was more developed or more compelling.

✓ Sample Assessment Questions - Theme

- Read the passage about _(topic)_ . Write a paragraph identifying the key details and explain how those details support the theme.

- What details from the text revealed the theme to you? Compare your initial analysis of the theme from the first few paragraphs of the selection to your final analysis at the end of the text.

- Write a summary paragraph which outlines what evidence from the text gave you the indication that the theme of the text is _(theme)_ . Include at least three examples from the text with an explanation of why these examples support the theme.

HOW TO TEACH THEME

GRADES 6-8

How to Teach Theme Using Informational Text

1

Take a look at the text features of the article

Headings, subheadings, italicized and bold type words, pictures, diagrams, labels, captions

2

Determine the purpose of the text

Entertain, persuade, inform, show cause/effect, compare/contrast, express an opinion

3

Take a look at the organization (structure) of the text

Written in chronological order (time, sequence)
Ideas in order of importance
Description

4

What are the three most important key details made in the text?

The three most important key details in ___(article title)___ are ___(detail 1)___ , ___(detail 2)___ , and ___(detail 3)___ .

5

What is the central idea of the text?

Write your three main points into one succinct sentence about the central idea.

6

To check your answer, you should be able to choose sentences that support and give details about your choice of the central idea or claim

My evidence to support my choice of the central claim of ___(article title)___ is ___(quotes of support)___ .

Student Frame for Analyzing Theme Using Two Pieces of Text

The first text, ___(text 1)___ , and the second text, ___(text 2)___ , are both about ___(central ideas or themes)___ .

They are similar because ___(how the texts are similar)___ . Both texts produce a complex account by

___(how the texts build complex accounts)___ . Both texts are different because ___(how the texts are different)___ .

Despite their differences, both texts build on the theme ___(theme)___ .

HOW TO TEACH THEME

GRADES 9-12

How to Teach Theme Using Informational Text

1	**Review text to identify text features** Identify type of source, headings, subheadings, main vocabulary, diagrams, pictures, statistics. How do these features immediately help orient you to the potential theme or central idea?
2	**Identify the purpose of the informational text** The author suggests the following about the ___(key idea 1)___ : ___(summary of author's supporting details)___ . The author further suggests the following about the ___(key idea 2)___ in the text: ___(summary of author's supporting details)___ . Explain how ___(key ideas)___ evolve over the course of the text. Cite textual evidence.
3	**Analyze the organization of the text** What choices did the author make in structuring the text so that the theme was highlighted?
4	**Identify the author's argument in the text** In ___(name the text)___ , the author argues that ___(the author's argument about the themes in the text)___ .
5	**Write a thesis statement** The themes and central ideas in this text, ___(name the text)___ , are ___(central ideas or themes)___ .
6	**To check your answer, you should be able to give details that support your choice of the central idea of the text** The multiple themes of this text are supported by the following evidence: ___(three supporting details)___ .

Student Frame for Analyzing Theme Using Two Pieces of Text

The first text, ___(text 1)___ , and the second text, ___(text 2)___ , are both about ___(central ideas or themes)___ .

They are similar because ___(how the texts are similar)___ . Both texts produce a complex account by

___(how the texts build complex accounts)___ . Both texts are different because ___(how the texts are different)___ .

Despite their differences, both texts build on the theme ___(theme)___ .

HOW TO TEACH FIGURATIVE LANGUAGE

Figurative language is when an author describes an object, event or scene by comparing it with something else. Oftentimes an author or speaker uses figurative language to dramatically emphasize or explain something.

LITERAL LANGUAGE
Taken at face value

For example: *Joe is a turtle.*

This means that we are literally referring to an actual turtle named Joe.

FIGURATIVE LANGUAGE
Using words to imply another meaning

For example: *Joe is a turtle...he always makes us late.*

This means that Joe is as slow as a turtle and makes his family late to events because he takes so long to get ready in the morning.

TYPES OF FIGURATIVE LANGUAGE

- Simile
- Alliteration
- Cliché
- Metaphor
- Onomatopoeia
- Idioms
- Personification
- Hyperbole

REASONS WHY AUTHORS USE FIGURATIVE LANGUAGE

- To add color
- To add drama
- To improve persuasiveness
- To provide clarity
- To be witty
- To break the monotony of speaking literally

HOW TO TEACH FIGURATIVE LANGUAGE

	ACTION STEPS
STEP 1	Teach students that an author uses figurative language to tell something without saying it directly. An example of figurative language is when I say to my friend in a very dramatic way, *"I am so tired, I think I might die!"* I am not literally going to die from exhaustion, but I am trying to make a dramatic point to my friend. I used figurative language, specifically hyperbole, to get my point across!
STEP 2	Give several more examples of figurative language such as: • Metaphor: *"He is a lion in battle!"* • Personification: *"My computer throws a fit every time I don't shut it down properly."* • Alliteration: *"Fred's friends fried Fritos for fun!"* • Onomatopoeia: *"They went splish-splashing down the waterslide."*
STEP 3	Now explain to students that there are eight types of figurative language that they will learn throughout the school year: simile, metaphor, personification, alliteration, onomatopoeia, hyperbole, cliché and idiom. Explain that oftentimes authors use figurative language to help the reader imagine what is happening in the text. The first one they'll study is simile.
STEP 4	Tell students that similes use the words "like" or "as" to compare things. These are the key words that help us recognize when the author has used simile to build an image or draw attention to a point.
STEP 5	Now say to students, *"I am going to read a paragraph that has three similes. I want you to watch as I model how to find the similes. It will be your turn to try it next!"*
STEP 6	Model the paragraph and think-aloud about the similes and how you identified them. Note for students why the author might have emphasized particular points within the text through the use of similes.
STEP 7	Tell students, *"Now it's your turn! Together, we are going to read the next paragraph - it has two similes that we'll identify."* Practice with at least three paragraphs before moving to Step 8.
STEP 8	Once students can identify similes, then model how similes impact the meaning of the text. Your model might sound like this: *"Hmmm...I really want to examine why the author chose to use the wording, 'Running Bear ran as fast as the wind to his grandmother's house, as if he had never run so fast before.' What I realize is that if the author had said, 'Running Bear ran fast to his grandmother's house,' I might've missed that he ran super fast!* *Also, I remember at the beginning of the text, the author described the wind as 'so fast and furious that it caused a howling noise and tipped over the teepees that had been standing for years.' The use of figurative language in this example really helped me understand that in comparing Running Bear to the wind, he was running faster than fast which showed how scared and concerned he really was."*
STEP 9	Continue Steps 1-8 with metaphor, personification, alliteration, onomatopoeia, hyperbole, cliché and idiom.

HOW TO TEACH FIGURATIVE LANGUAGE

GRADES K-2

Student Friendly Definitions for Figurative Language

A **simile** is a phrase that compares two things or people, using the clue words "like" or "as"

> *The game was as boring as watching paint dry.*

A **metaphor** is a phrase used to identify something that clearly is not true

> *Emily is a fox.*

Personification is when human qualities are given to animals or things

> *The stairs groaned when we climbed them.*

Alliteration is a group of words that start with the same beginning sound and are sometimes called tongue twisters

> *Keegan's kangaroo kept kicking kids.*

Onomatopoeia is when a word actually means the same or similar to how it sounds when you say it

> *The campfire crackled and popped.*

Hyperbole is an exaggeration usually used to be funny or draw attention to a topic

> *My grandpa is older than dirt!*

A **cliché** is a saying used to express a popular idea and is used again and again

> *When life gives you lemons, make lemonade.*

An **idiom** is a phrase that cannot be taken literally

> *She was as sick as a dog after riding the roller coaster.*

Grab and Go Figurative Language Prompts and Questions

1. Model for students where in the text the author used figurative language: The author, ___(author)___ , used ___(type of figurative language)___ in the sentence ___(sentence)___ .

2. Model for students how you know the author used figurative language in the text: I can tell that the author used ___(type of figurative language)___ because ___(how you know)___ . *Example: I can tell the author used a simile in this text because he compares the slow moving game where no points have been scored to watching paint dry. Games with little action can be boring. If you were watching paint dry that would be boring too.*

3. Practice with students the alliteration found in the text. First, read the alliteration. Next, have students identify the beginning sound in the words of the alliteration. Lastly, guide them in reciting the alliteration and discuss why the author would have chosen to use it at this point in the text.

4. How does the use of ___(type of figurative language)___ help you to visualize the setting (and/or the characters) of the text better?

5. When the author uses ___(type of figurative language)___ how does it make the text more interesting? What would it sound like if the author chose not to include ___(example of figurative language)___ ?

6. Identify the author's use of ___(type of figurative language)___ in the text and think aloud for students why its use is effective.

7. Identify with students the author's use of ___(type of figurative language)___ . Ask: How do you know the author used ___(personification)___ ? What were the clues in the text?

8. Can an ___(animal or object)___ really ___(human quality given to the animal or object)___ ?

9. I see the words "like" and "as" to describe ___(character)___ in the text. Is this a simile or metaphor?

10. Why do authors use ___(type of figurative language)___ ?

HOW TO TEACH FIGURATIVE LANGUAGE

GRADES 3-5

Student Friendly Definitions for Figurative Language

A **simile** is a type of metaphor, a phrase that compares two things or people

Her lips are soft, like a pillow.

A **metaphor** is a phrase used to make a hidden comparison to two things that are like one another

My brother was boiling mad!

Personification is when human qualities are given to animals or things

The moon played hide and seek with the clouds.

Alliteration is a sequence of words that start with the same beginning sound

Heather heaves heavy hammers.

Onomatopoeia is a word that, when spoken, sounds like the meaning of the word

Drip, drip, drip went the rain, whoosh went the wind, and whoo-whoo went the owl in the night.

Hyperbole is an exaggeration usually used to be funny or to give the situation more emphasis

If I don't get a smart phone for my birthday, I'll just die.

A **cliché** is a phrase or expression that has been used so often that it is no longer original

Haste makes waste.

An **idiom** is a phrase that cannot be taken literally and is often used to describe something or someone

The boy was as sick as a dog, even after he got his yearly flu shot!

Grab and Go Figurative Language Prompts and Questions

1. Where in the text did the author use ___*(type of figurative language)*___?

2. How do you know that the author used ___*(type of figurative language)*___? Are there clues? If so, what are they?

3. How does the use of ___*(type of figurative language)*___ help you to visualize the character(s) or setting?

4. How does using ___*(type of figurative language)*___ add expression or emphasis in this paragraph?

5. Why do you think that the author chose to use one form of figurative language over another in this passage? Would the meaning have been altered if a different form of figurative language was used here?

6. The words in the phrase ___*(read the phrase from the text)*___ literally mean ___*(what the words literally mean)*___, but what do they mean in the context of this sentence?

7. What does the phrase ___*(figurative language phrase from the text)*___ literally mean?

8. How does the meaning of the text change if we take the ___*(type of figurative language)*___ literally?

9. What context clues do you need to use to figure out ___*(example of figurative language)*___? Does the text give you clues to figure out what the author meant?

10. How does the figurative language used in this text give you an idea of the time period? Are there examples of figurative language that we would not use today? Why does the author include them?

HOW TO TEACH FIGURATIVE LANGUAGE

GRADES 6-8

Student Friendly Definitions for Figurative Language

A **simile** is a comparison of often unrelated things using the words "like" or "as"

Grandpa lounged on the raft in the middle of the pool like an old battleship.

A **metaphor** is a hidden or implied comparison of two things that are not typically thought to have a connection

Her hair was a flowing golden river streaming down her shoulders.

Personification is when something that is not human is given human-like qualities

The cactus saluted any visitor brave enough to travel the scorched land.

Alliteration is repeated consonant sounds at the beginning of several words in a phrase or sentence

The beautiful bouquet blossomed in the bright sun.

Onomatopoeia is a word that imitates the natural sound of the thing it is describing

The cash register popped open with a heartwarming ca-ching.

Hyperbole is exaggerating, often in a humorous way, to make a particular point

Forget knocking it out of the park, Frank can knock a baseball off the continent!

A **cliché** is a phrase or expression that has been used so often that it is no longer original

The movie kept me on the edge of my seat.

An **idiom** is an expression that cannot be understood from the individual meanings of its elements

Bobby would have played ball until the cows came home if it hadn't been for Suzie dragging him home for dinner.

Grab and Go Figurative Language Prompts and Questions

1. Explain the impact the author made by using ___*(figurative language)*___ at this point in the text.

2. How does the author utilize the ___*(figurative language)*___ in this paragraph/section to move the plot in a new direction?

3. Describe how the author uses ___*(figurative language)*___ in this section of the text to change the tone of the piece.

4. Cite three different places in the text that encourage the reader to visualize. Discuss how figurative language plays a role.

5. Describe the impression the author makes with sound by utilizing onomatopoeia in this section of text.

6. How does the metaphor used in ___*(title of text)*___ add to or change the meaning of the piece?

7. Why does the author use alliteration in the story? What would the reader miss if the repetition was not included in the text?

8. Why does ___*(character)*___ respond using figurative language in paragraph __*(#)*__ ?

9. Which words in paragraphs __*(#)*__ and __*(#)*__ help the reader understand what ___*(figurative language)*___ means?

10. Look at this group of words. What is the meaning of the phrase? Explain why you think the author chose this ___*(figurative language)*___.

HOW TO TEACH FIGURATIVE LANGUAGE

GRADES 9-12

Student Friendly Definitions for Figurative Language

A **simile** is a comparison of different things or ideas by using the words "like" or "as"

The water in the cooler gurgled like a happy baby.

A **metaphor** is the comparison of unlike things or ideas showing similar qualities

Three pines strained darkly, runners in a race unseen by any.

Personification is the attribution of human characteristics to inanimate objects, natural forces, animals or ideas

Distant mountains call, "come closer."

Alliteration is the repetition of initial consonant sounds within a phrase or sentence

Pete pecked at the protruding pencil point.

Onomatopoeia is a word or words that sound like the action or thing they describe or represent

When he sat down, the young boy squished the unfortunate critter in his pocket.

Hyperbole is an exaggeration used to provoke strong emotion, to create humor or to make a point

She sliced him a piece of cake so thin it floated to the plate.

A **cliché** is an expression that has been used so often that its meaning and impact are no longer effective

She was as tough as nails during the contentious negotiations.

An **idiom** is an expression that is understood only by those familiar with the language

"Next year you'll sing a different tune," she cried out as she slammed the car door.

Grab and Go Figurative Language Prompts and Questions

1. Identify the specific connotative and figurative language addressed by the author of the text. The author uses and refines the meaning of ___*(figurative language)*___ in the text by ___*(how author uses figurative language)*___.

2. Give students a copy of *Hope is the Thing with Feathers* by Emily Dickenson. What metaphor does Dickenson present in the first stanza? How is the metaphor developed throughout the poem?

3. Give students a copy of *The Seven Ages of Man* by William Shakespeare. The speaker compares the world to a stage. What does this comparison imply about the speaker's view of life?

4. How does figurative language help you understand characters and events more deeply than if the author used literal language and wording?

5. The author uses ___*(figurative language)*___ to change the tone of the piece. Explain how.

6. How does the meaning or effect of repeated words change over time? Does the use of alliteration propel the plot or main points in the text? What purpose does it serve?

7. Give examples of simile, metaphor, personification and hyperbole to students. Ask them to identify the figure of speech in each, explain its meaning and describe the mood it conveys.

8. Give students an example of a simile. Have students change it into a metaphor. What would need to be done to change them to reflect personification and hyperbole?

9. Which figures of speech do you find the most compelling? Explain your preferences and give examples.

10. How does the use of figurative language in this piece unify the author's message or reveal the theme? Do the devices serve the author's purpose, in your opinion? Give specific examples from the text in your response.

HOW TO TEACH POINT OF VIEW

Point of View is the perspective from which a speaker or writer tells a narrative or presents information to the reader. Point of View is presented in three ways: first person, second person and third person.

FIRST PERSON
*By the narrator:
I, me, mine*

SECOND PERSON
*By the author:
you, your*

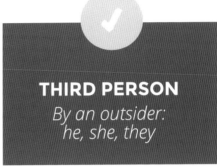

THIRD PERSON
*By an outsider:
he, she, they*

Why Authors Use First Person

- Immediately connects the reader to the protagonist because he is in his head

- Creates a sense of believability because the story is being told first-hand

- The reader knows exactly who is telling the story from the beginning

Why Authors Use Second Person

- Surprises the reader and grabs attention simply because this point of view is so rarely used

- Gets personal, because the author uses "you" and refers directly to the reader

- Prompts the reader to connect to his own personal memories and experiences

Why Authors Use Third Person

- Most narrative pieces are written in third person, so it is traditional

- Allows the reader to get to know multiple characters throughout the text

- Gives the reader a peek into many vantage points at the same time

How to Teach Students to Critically Think About Text

HOW TO TEACH POINT OF VIEW

STEP 1

Teach the definition of point of view and why it is important for comprehension (refer to "Why Authors Use" from the front of this tab).

STEP 2

Model a paragraph from the text and show students how you use the language of the text (I, me, mine, you, your, he, she, they) to determine the point of view.

STEP 3

Use three different paragraphs from other pieces of text and model the language/key words of the text to determine the point of view for additional practice.

STEP 4

Once students are firm on the skill of identifying the point of view, then move to modeling how and why point of view matters in the text.

"Ladies and gentlemen, today we are going to dig into a short story about a man's visit to his dentist and how his enemy, the dentist, nearly ruins him. I'm going to read the first couple of paragraphs to you and then model the what, why and how of point of view. Then it'll be your turn!"

Read a short portion of the text to students.

"Hmmm...I know that this short story is written in the first person because the narrator uses the terms 'I' and 'me' to refer to the action. Now my next step is to ask myself why the author's choice of first person is important to my understanding of the short story.

First, I look at the paragraph where the narrator is describing the immense pain that he's in because his enemy, the dentist, wouldn't give him numbing medicine. His wording 'I could have died. In fact, I wanted to die right there on the table,' is so powerful that I could literally feel his pain. I wonder if this is why the author chose to use first person - I feel like I'm actually there!"

Repeat this step at least three times before moving ahead to Step 5.

STEP 5

Use another short story for guided practice with the class. While students are practicing in small groups or individually, provide feedback on linking their responses back to examples from the text. Repeat this step until firm.

STEP 6

When students are firm on the identification and analysis of point of view, have them regularly identify and analyze the point of view as a pre-reading strategy.

How to Teach Students to Critically Think About Text

HOW TO TEACH POINT OF VIEW

GRADES K-2

Questions for Identifying Point of View

- Model for students how key words from the text show the point of view.

- Model for students that the text's point of view shifts across the story and explain where this change takes place.

- Model for students how the illustration adds to a reader's understanding of the author's point of view.

- Model for students how a reader uses the title, the illustrations/photos, and the text to understand the point of view.

- Model for students how the author and the illustrator shared the same point of view in the text. (Only choose this with a text written and illustrated by different people).

Questions for Analyzing Characters and Point of View

- What is the main character's point of view?

- Model for students how the point of view would be different from the perspective of another character in the text.

- Retell the story from the 1st, 2nd, and 3rd person point of view.

- How does the point of view affect how the reader feels about the characters in the story?

Questions for Analyzing Multiple Points of View

- How do the two stories about _____ *(topic/theme)* _____ change because of the author's choice of point of view?

- Model for students how to compare the two texts about _____ *(topic)* _____. Demonstrate how the two different points of view change how information is shared about _____ *(topic)* _____.

- Citing evidence from the text, model for students how your point of view about the topic differs from the author's point of view.

Questions for Analyzing the Impact of Point of View

- Does the point of view offered in the text change how you feel about _____ *(topic)* _____?

- Model for students how the point of view causes you to feel _____ *(feeling)* _____ when _____ *(examples from the text)* _____.

- Model for students that before reading _____ *(title of text)* _____, your opinion on the topic was _____ *(opinion on the topic)* _____, but after reading the text from the _____ *(1st, 2nd, or 3rd person point of view)* _____ you feel _____ *(current opinion on the topic)* _____. Have students discuss how their opinions stayed the same or changed after listening to the two texts.

HOW TO TEACH POINT OF VIEW

GRADES 3-5

Questions for Identifying Point of View

- The point of view in the text _____(title of text)_____ is _____(1st, 2nd, or 3rd person point of view)_____. Key words that indicate point of view in the text are _____(key words from the text)_____.

- The text is written from the 3rd person point of view. How would the text be similar if it were written from the 1st person? How would it be different?

- Can you tell how the author's purpose for writing _____(title of text)_____ is based on the point of view? Explain.

- Based on the title, can you tell what the point of view is likely to be? Why do you think this?

- How does the point of view change from the beginning of the text to the end of the text? How do you know?

Questions for Analyzing Characters and Point of View

- The point of view from the main character is _____(point of view)_____.

- How does the point of view give you insight about _____(other character)_____?

- If the story had been told from _____(other character)_____ then _____(describe how point of view changes)_____.

- How does the text written from the first person point of view show bias or judgment?

Questions for Analyzing Multiple Points of View

- Compare the two texts about _____(topic)_____. How do the two different points of view change how information is shared about _____(topic)_____?

- How does your point of view about the topic differ from the author's point of view?

- Retell the story from a different point of view than what the author used. How does the theme or central idea change?

- Which opinion article about _____(topic)_____ is most similar to the author's point of view in _____(title of text)_____?

Questions for Analyzing the Impact of Point of View

- How does the point of view in the text affect your opinion about _____(topic)_____?

- How does the point of view in the text cause the reader to dislike _____(the main character's actions)_____?

- The point of view causes me to feel _____(feeling)_____ because _____(reason)_____.

- Before reading _____(title of text)_____ my thoughts or opinion of _____(topic)_____ was _____(opinion on topic)_____, but after reading the text from the _____(1st, 2nd, or 3rd person point of view)_____ I feel _____(opinion now on the topic)_____.

- The _____(1st, 2nd, or 3rd person point of view)_____ used in the text makes the story more/less persuasive because _____(reason 1)_____, _____(reason 2)_____.

HOW TO TEACH POINT OF VIEW

GRADES 6-8

Questions for Identifying Point of View

- The story, ____(story)____, is told from the ____(1st, 2nd, or 3rd person point of view)____. I know this because the author uses ____(examples from the text)____ language in the text.

- This author, ____(author)____, is from ____(country outside of U.S.)____. His treatment of ____(culture, experience, or perspective given by author in text)____ lets me know that the story is being told from the following point of view: ____(point of view)____.

- What are the authors' stated or implied point of view and purpose in relation to this subject?

- The author uses the word ____(word)____ in this text. Using this key word as a reference, what is the author's point of view?

Questions for Analyzing Characters and Point of View

- Consider how learning ____(character)____'s thoughts contribute to your understanding of ____(his)____ character. How would your reaction to ____(character)____ be different if you didn't know what ____(character)____ was thinking and feeling?

- What details in the story support the view that ____(character 1)____ is a romantic and ____(character 2)____ is a realist? Compare your responses with your peers.

- Since the text, ____(title of text)____, is told from the 3rd person point of view, the narrator relays thoughts of several characters. Did knowing these inner thoughts affect your opinion of another character? Explain your answer with evidence from the text.

- Compare and contrast ____(character 1)____ and ____(character 2)____. How does the author's choice of point of view play a role in your analysis?

Questions for Analyzing Multiple Points of View

- The narrator does not convey ____(character)____'s thoughts. The narrator does give the reader clues about how ____(character)____ thinks and feels. What are these clues, and what do they tell you about ____(character)____?

- With a 1st person narrator, the reader sees the story unfold though the eyes of one character. Consider how ____(character)____ views the story's characters and events. Would a 3rd person point of view have presented a more engaging depiction of ____(event or topic)____? Explain why or why not.

- What does the author reveal about the narrator's character through his own and others' speech, thoughts, feelings and actions. How much self-knowledge does the narrator have? Does the narrator change during the story? If so, how?

- What does the narrator reveal about the ____(motivations)____ of each of the characters? How might this story be different if the narrator were not omniscient?

- Identify two passages in the story that show the narrator is omniscient. What insights by the narrator particularly strike you? Describe how the story might have been different if it had been told in the 3rd person point of view?

HOW TO TEACH POINT OF VIEW

GRADES 9-12

Questions for Identifying Point of View

- Where and when does the author distinguish between what the characters say and what they think?

- What question is the author trying to answer or address in the text? How does the author go about expressing this point of view?

- Identify the point of view from which the text, ___(title of text)___, is told. How might your impression of ___(character)___ be different if you didn't receive such detailed descriptions of his thoughts and feelings?

Questions for Analyzing Characters and Point of View

- In what ways does ___(narrator)___'s description of ___(character)___ tell you about their relationship? Cite evidence from text.

- How would you describe the narrator's tone in the description of ___(character)___? How does this description change how you feel about ___(character)___?

- A round character is one who is complex and highly developed, displaying a variety of different traits in his personality. A flat character is not highly developed. He usually has one outstanding trait or role and exists mainly to advance the plot of the text. Identify one round character and one flat character in the text. Then explain how each fits the criteria above, give very specific details.

- Compare a character from two literary works. Which one has a more remarkable personality? Explain why.

Questions for Analyzing Multiple Points of View

- What event or issue is the subject of these different texts? How does each author present this information?

- How would you characterize and compare the authors' different perspectives on this subject?

- What criteria would you use to assess the authors' claims, reasons or evidence? How might the information be better presented to persuade the audience? Does the author use multiple points of view to support the theme/central idea?

- How would the end of the text be different if it were told exclusively from 1st person point of view? Explain.

- Examine different points of view on historical events by listing the claims, reasons, and evidence for those acts or events.

Questions for Analyzing the Impact of Point of View

- How does the author use the 3rd person limited point of view to create ___(mood/theme/atmosphere)___? Cite textual evidence.

- Consider what you learned about ___(central idea/theme)___. How do the narrator's comments affect your impression of the ___(central idea/theme)___?

- Generate words that characterize the style of writing. Explain how these words are shaped by the point of view *Example: How the point of view guided the writer to make certain choices about diction, tone, and setting.*

HOW TO TEACH ANALYSIS

GRADES K-2

Action Steps	Focus Questions and Prompts
1 Teach and model for students how to study the introduction and conclusion paragraphs and recognize any changes in the character	• Compare and contrast the main character from the beginning of the text to the end of the text: 　• Use the illustrations and the first few sentences to describe the main character. 　• Use the illustrations and the last few sentences to describe the main character. 　• At the beginning of the text ___(main character's name)___ was ___(description)___, but at the end of the text ___(main character)___ was ___(description)___. • The main character, ___(main character)___, at the end of the text is ___(description)___. Is that how he would be described in the beginning of the text? Why or why not? • How does ___(author)___ introduce the characters in ___(title of text)___?
2 Teach and model how to study the main character and his patterns throughout the text	• What caused ___(main character)___ to change from the beginning to the end of the text? • Identify the place in the text where the character begins to change from how he was at the beginning of ___(title of text)___. • What details or clues in the text help you identify that the character is changing?
3 Teach and model how to scrutinize the relationships between the main characters	• This text has more than one main character. Who are the important characters in the text ___(title of text)___? • Do the characters act or talk differently when they are with each other than when they're not with each other? • How are the characters connected to each other and what do they have in common? • Do all of the characters feel or react in the same way about the problem in the text? Explain.
4 Teach and model how to determine the author's use of the antagonist to build the theme	• Who is the antagonist in the text? • How does ___(antagonist)___ treat ___(main character)___? Give examples from the text. • As ___(main character)___ changes, how does ___(antagonist)___ change across the text? • What are the motives of the antagonist?
5 Teach and model how to recognize and highlight repetitions that are potentially meaningful	• What words/phrase/chant is (are) repeated throughout the text? • What do the repeated words/phrase/chant mean to the character or the setting? • How would the text change if the repeated words/phrase/chant were deleted? • Are the words that are repeated/chanted figurative language? If so, what type?
6 Teach and model how to chart the progress of the character from beginning to end, particularly noting his actions in the climax	• First ___(main character)___ was ___(description)___. • The problem in the text was ___(problem statement)___. • Then, because ___(problem)___, the main character ___(actions main character took to solve the problem)___. • At the end of the text ___(main character)___ was ___(description)___.

HOW TO TEACH ANALYSIS

GRADES 3-5

Action Steps	Focus Questions and Prompts
1 Teach and model for students how to study the introduction and conclusion paragraphs and recognize any changes in the character	• Who is the main character and what is said about that character at the beginning of the text? • The author introduces ____*(main character)*____ by ____*(details from the text)*____ . • Which characters are most important and complex in the story and why? • The ____*(main character)*____ is dealing with the issue of ____*(theme or central idea)*____ .
2 Teach and model how to study the main character and his patterns throughout the text	• The main character, ____*(main character)*____ , interacts with ____*(another character)*____ by ____*(describe in detail)*____ . • The main character, *(main character)*, engages in the following activities: *(activities)* . • The main character, ____*(main character)*____ , does ____*(action)*____ and this impacts the character, ____*(another character)*____ , by ____*(impact on this character)*____ .
3 Teach and model how to scrutinize the relationships between the main characters	• The main character is connected to ____*(main character)*____ by ____*(describe relationship)*____ . Continue with all characters in the story. • What happens to the main character and the other characters in the story? • Which parts of the text are unclear or vague? Do you think this is on purpose? • What important detail or event influences the characters and their relationship the most?
4 Teach and model how to determine the author's use of the antagonist to build the theme	• Explain who the antagonist is and his position in the text. • How does the main character handle the situation with the antagonist? • How does the author's decision about the main character's development impact the story's meaning? Could the author have handled it differently? • What does the main character want and why? What do these desires tell us about the character?
5 Teach and model how to recognize and highlight repetitions that are potentially meaningful	• Which specific word choices are interesting or important? • Does the author use these words literally or figuratively? How do you know? • How do words contribute to the author's tone? Give examples from the text. • What specialized words are necessary to know in order to understand key concepts?
6 Teach and model how to chart the progress of the character from beginning to end, particularly noting his actions in the climax	• What conclusions can you draw about the characters' development from these different sources? • What information in each source best relates or addresses the topic?

HOW TO TEACH ANALYSIS

Analysis is when a reader methodically examines a piece of text in order to understand, explain and interpret its meaning.

A SIMPLE ANALYSIS

A simple analysis requires the reader to:

1. Study the introduction and conclusion

2. Study the main character's patterns

3. Study the relationships between the characters

4. Study the antagonist

5. Study repetitions within the text

6. Study the characters' actions at pivotal parts of the story

HOW TO TEACH ANALYSIS

	ACTION STEPS	CONSIDERATIONS
STEP 1	Teach and model for students how to study the introduction and conclusion paragraphs and recognize any changes in the character	• How is the main character introduced? • What are your initial thoughts about the main character? • What important information does the author give in the conclusion?
STEP 2	Teach and model how to study the character and his patterns throughout the text	Examine the character by looking at: • His actions • Activities he is engaged in • His style of talk and discussion with other characters • The actions of other characters in relation to the main character
STEP 3	Teach and model how to scrutinize the relationships between the characters	• Draw a table or graphic that highlights the relationships between the main character and other characters • Analyze the trends of the relationships and how they shape the plot or theme
STEP 4	Teach and model how to determine the author's use of the antagonist to build the theme	• Examine the relationship the antagonist has with the main character • Examine the relationship the antagonist has with other characters • Note the author's use of dialogue between the main character and the antagonist • Highlight specific words or language that the author uses with particular characters
STEP 5	Teach and model how to recognize and highlight repetitions that are potentially meaningful	Highlight those areas within the text where there are repetitions: • Phrases • Statements • Words • Examples
STEP 6	Teach and model how to chart the progress of the character from beginning to end, particularly noting his actions in the climax	Chart the main character's progression and reactions to the addition of other characters, situations and problems

How to Teach Students to Critically Think About Text

HOW TO TEACH ANALYSIS

GRADES 6-8

	Action Steps	Focus Questions and Prompts
1	Teach and model for students how to study the introduction and conclusion paragraphs and recognize any changes in the character	• The author first introduces the character and uses the verbs _(verb 1)_ , _(verb 2)_ and _(verb 3)_ to describe him. What do the verbs say about the character, at first glance? • How does the initial setting shed light on the main character when you first meet him? • If you could describe the progression of the main character from the beginning to the end, what word would you use and why? Give examples from the text.
2	Teach and model how to study the main character and his patterns throughout the text	• Make five boxes on a piece of paper and chunk the text into five logical pieces. In each of the boxes, list one adjective describing the main character in that portion of the text. What patterns do you notice, if any? • As you analyze the moves that the character makes throughout the first half of the text, what do you notice about his habits? What do the habits say about his personality? • Are there any out of character behaviors that the main character exhibits? If so, what are the circumstances?
3	Teach and model how to scrutinize the relationships between the main characters	• Write all of the characters' names on the left-hand side of the paper and on the right-hand side of the paper (you will write each name twice). Draw connecting lines from one character to another that indicates a relationship or connection. Which characters are most connected to the others? Which characters have little to no connection to the others? What does that tell you? • Imagine that _(character)_ was not present in the narrative. What impact would that have on the other characters? Why did the author choose to include this character and what role does he play? • How do you think the author feels toward the main characters? Why?
4	Teach and model how to determine the author's use of the antagonist to build the theme	• Describe the setting and the mood when the antagonist entered the picture. What did the author want you to feel at that moment? Give specific evidence from the text. • The antagonist exists to show a different side of the main character. How does the antagonist's character provide a different look at the main character? • The author chooses to use the words _(word 1)_ and _(word 2)_ to describe the antagonist. He uses _(adjective 1)_ and _(adjective 2)_ to describe the protagonist. Why do you think the author chose those words in particular? Do they have a connection or a significant non-connection?
5	Teach and model how to recognize and highlight repetitions that are potentially meaningful	• Authors often repeat phrasing or vocabulary within the text to draw attention to a particular point. What repetitions do you notice and what significance do they have? • The author has the main character return to this setting again and again: _(setting)_ . Why is this repetition important in building the theme? • Let's take a closer look at the phrasing that the author uses in paragraph _(#)_ versus paragraph _(#)_ . Why do you think the author wrote those paragraphs so similarly? What is happening there that you need to pay attention to?
6	Teach and model how to chart the progress of the character from beginning to end, particularly noting his actions in the climax	• Make a simple T-Chart and down the left-hand side list four adjectives the author uses to describe the main character at the beginning of the text and down the right-hand side, list four adjectives to describe the character at the end of the text. What do you notice?

HOW TO TEACH ANALYSIS

GRADES 9-12

	Action Steps	Focus Questions and Prompts
1	Teach and model for students how to study the introduction and conclusion paragraphs and recognize any changes in the character	• What is said about the main character at the beginning, middle and end of the story? What is unsaid? • How are the events in the story arranged – and to what end? • How are the characters introduced and developed? Are there similar or different approaches for each character? • Which events are most important to the main character and why?
2	Teach and model how to study the main character and his patterns throughout the text	• Describe the setting. How does the choice affect the story's meaning or impact? If the setting was different, would it change the outcome? • What evidence from the text supports your claim about the meaning and importance of characters, events and the evolving relationship between them? • How are the characters connected to one another? • How do the characters change over the course of the text from beginning to end? • Which of the author's decisions most affect the elements of the narrative and how they develop or connect to each other over time?
3	Teach and model how to scrutinize the relationships between the main characters	• Explain the plot and which characters are most affected by the central idea. • Develop a continuum of important events to evaluate which details are most important in the story. • What facts, events or relationships are critical to the narrative? • How are the relationships in one account of events different from another account? • What does the main character need from other characters?
4	Teach and model how to determine the author's use of the antagonist to build the theme	• Describe the complex relationship between the antagonist and the main character. • What impact do the antagonist's actions have on other key character(s)? • What evidence in the text is most credible to the story line and development of characters?
5	Teach and model how to recognize and highlight repetitions that are potentially meaningful	• Which key words have multiple meanings in the text? • What are the different possible meanings of _(word/phrase)_ as it is used in the text? • How do the author's words or phrases contribute to the meaning of the text? To the outcome? • How do the words chosen reflect or respond to the setting, occasion or audience? • What is the cumulative impact of the author's chosen words on the purpose, setting, meaning and tone? Give examples from the text.
6	Teach and model how to chart the progress of the character from beginning to end, particularly noting his actions in the climax	• Describe which events in the character's life are emphasized in particular and why. • How are events relating to the protagonist arranged and why? • When you analyze the character's actions in the climax, what behavioral patterns do you notice?

HOW TO TEACH DISCUSSION

GRADES K-2

Student Discussion Checklist

✔ I wrote down one question to ask during the discussion

✔ I know three details about ___(topic, character, setting)___ that I learned from the text

✔ I have written down three details about the main character of the text

✔ I have written down one question that I'm still wondering about after reading the text

✔ I am prepared to retell someone else's opinion/point about ___(topic)___

✔ I made eye contact with various members of the group as I spoke

Teacher Preparation List for Leading a Discussion

_____ Ensure the students have access to the text during the discussion

_____ Provide students with picture cards that match the text to assist them in discussion

_____ Before the discussion begins, give students two minutes to write down a question about the topic or text

_____ Prompt students with a sentence starter such as: _The change in the character was caused by..._

_____ Prepare two to three open-ended questions to ignite the discussion.
_For example: What do you think of the solution to the problem of ___(problem)___? What new ideas did you learn from reading this text?_

_____ Prompt students to refer to other responses as they add to the conversation

_____ Have students do a quick-draw about the main character, setting, or problem following the discussion

HOW TO TEACH DISCUSSION

GRADES 3-5

Student Discussion Checklist

✔ I've read the text and am prepared to discuss how I agree or disagree with the point of view the author shared in the text

✔ I wrote down the main idea and three supporting details to use during the class discussion

✔ I have one question to ask about the topic, character, setting or theme

✔ I have written down a confusing sentence or phrase that I'd like my class to discuss

✔ I know how I feel about this topic and can use the text to support me during the discussion

✔ I avoid responding only to my teacher during a discussion and purposely make eye contact with everyone in my group

Teacher Preparation List for Leading a Discussion

_____ During the discussion write down student comments on chart paper and allow students to refer to and keep track of what was already stated (refer to the "Note-taking" tab)
  • Model how to retell what was just shared and link to it by adding a differing opinion, asking a question, or giving an example from the text

_____ Have a set of 'how' and 'why' questions prepared to spark conversation as it lags
  • Require students to refer back to their text and if a student reads word for word from the text, prompt them to retell what was just read in their own words

_____ If the discussion stalls, try these steps:
  • Ask students to show, by thumbs up or thumbs down, if they agree or disagree with the solution to the problem as presented in the text
  • Divide the group into those who agree and those who disagree
  • Then, allow for a three minute small group discussion as to why they agree or disagree
  • Bring the whole group back together and prompt them to restart the discussion

_____ Pre-select a paragraph or section of text for students to re-read as an energizer

_____ Prompt students to share how this text connects to another text that was previously read

HOW TO TEACH DISCUSSION

GRADES 6-8

Student Discussion Checklist and Response Frames

✓ I carefully organized my notes and have written a summary statement about the text (refer to the "Note-taking" tab)

✓ I jotted down three probing questions that I can use for follow-up during the discussion

✓ I am prepared to use at least three to four vocabulary words from the text during the discussion as a way to focus the information I contribute

✓ Sentence frame: I heard ___(student)___ say ___(summary of comments)___ made about ___(topic)___ . I agree with this statement because ___(reason)___ . Or I disagree with this statement because ___(reason)___ .

✓ Sentence frame: ___(student 1)___ and ___(student 2)___ have stated opposing views on the ___(topic)___ . From the evidence presented, I believe that ___(student)___ gave the most accurate account and here are at least three reasons why: ___(reason 1)___ , ___(reason 2)___ and ___(reason 3)___ .

Teacher Preparation List for Leading a Discussion

_____ Model for students how to gather information during a discussion by pausing and noting two things: what was said and how it impacts the students' notes or prior thinking on the topic

_____ After you have modeled how to gather information for several weeks, choose a different group each week to lead the class discussion

_____ Set students up with a simple self and peer grading system that they will use post-discussion: 3 = Met all of the criteria for discussion, 2 = Met partial criteria for discussion, 1 = Met little criteria for discussion

_____ Give students ample time to get organized for the discussion and require them to be prepared with at last two questions they can add to a stalled conversation

_____ Share with students the ways that they can bring attention to their point and how you expect them to incorporate these ideas into their discussions: varying voice levels, repeating information or pausing after an important point

_____ Plan for a two to three minute debriefing where you discuss: What went well (with examples), what did not go so well (with examples) and how to fix-up the discussion in the future

HOW TO TEACH DISCUSSION

GRADES 9-12

Student Discussion Checklist and Response Frames

✔ Prior to the discussion, I determined how I will structure my notes and have summarized important points should a discrepancy arise

✔ I weave in various students' ideas to either refute or substantiate a claim

✔ When I determine that there are discrepancies in an argument or discussion, I will use this sentence frame to share my ideas: After carefully scrutinizing the ___*(evidence provided by student)*___, I believe that there are discrepancies, such as: ___*(details)*___. These discrepancies are significant because ___*(impact of discrepancies and cite the text)*___.

✔ While I am listening to other speakers during the discussion, I will provide a brief summary by using this frame: Based upon ___*(quote from discussion)*___, I determined that ___*(student/author)*___'s view/stance on ___*(topic/text)*___ was ___*(student's stance)*___.

✔ When I analyze the tone of the discussion, I will use this frame: ___*(Student)*___ is ___*(calm/hostile/sympathetic)*___ toward the topic because ___*(opinion/evidence from discussion)*___.

Teacher Preparation List for Leading a Discussion

_____ Post a list of follow-up questions that challenge another speaker's evidence or reasoning

_____ Prepare alternatives for discussions such as videoconferencing or chat room discussions for student collaboration (refer to the "Technology" tab)

_____ Demonstrate how to identify discrepancies, explain your process and have students apply the techniques independently

_____ Show students how to break down the logic of an argument to determine whether the premise is true or not (refer to the "Argument/Opinion" tab)

_____ Model for students how to use a pro/con sheet to sort information before, during and after discussion

_____ Model for students a problem/solution T-Chart to use during discussions to organize information received from participants

_____ Explicitly teach where, in a discussion, students should use formal and informal speech and how both can be used to further their discussion when used appropriately

HOW TO TEACH PRESENTATION OF INFORMATION & IDEAS

*A **presentation** is when a student verbally shares information through a logical, thorough process, designed to educate listeners on topics, findings or themes.*

DESCRIPTION OF EACH STEP

1	Teach students how to understand the scope of the presentation by having them identify the task, audience and purpose for the presentation prior to starting (refer to the "Decode a Prompt" tab)
2	Teach students how to gather relevant information
3	Teach students how to create recordings, drawings and multimedia to enhance their content
4	Teach students how to coherently outline their presentation and create opportunities for interaction with the audience
5	Teach students how to speak audibly, change their voice pattern/volume for emphasis, repeat important points and make eye contact
6	Teach students how to ask relevant follow-up questions and provide feedback to the presenter

How to Teach Students to Research

1. Teacher shares at least three research topics or ideas for students to consider

2. Students begin broad research and journal about a couple of interesting ideas and topics

3. Students jot down three to five questions about the topics that they would like to answer

4. Students narrow down their research and develop a question that is of great interest to them about one of the topics

5. Students gather resources to answer their question and begin to cross-check information using multiple sources

6. Students synthesize the information they have researched and outline the form of the presentation

7. Students determine what multi-media sources they will use to enhance the presentation

8. Students present the question and findings to a group or class

HOW TO TEACH PRESENTATION OF INFORMATION & IDEAS

PRESENTATION RESOURCES

EXAMPLES OF MULTIMEDIA

PowerPoint presentation

Video demonstrations

Audio interviews

Web page creation

Digital collage creation

EXAMPLES OF INTERACTION WITH THE AUDIENCE

Ask the audience to take notes

Ask the audience to turn to a partner and discuss

Ask the audience to submit questions/ responses on a sticky note

Ask the audience to create a visual representation of what they are learning

Ask the audience to dramatize a particular process as you share it

EXAMPLES OF FOLLOW-UP QUESTIONS

What are two points that surprised you and why?

What is one point that you still have questions about?

What information will you go and use right away?

How does this information connect to other presentations you've heard on the topic?

Does this presentation spark you to do additional research? Why or why not?

HOW TO GIVE FEEDBACK TO A PRESENTER

____ Did the presenter explain ideas coherently and logically?

____ Did the presenter include all of the necessary components of the presentation?

____ Did the presenter's body language enhance or detract from the information?

____ Did the presenter keep eye contact with the audience throughout the presentation?

____ Did the presenter's voice project confidence? Did the presenter use different tones for emphasis?

____ Did the presenter's multimedia enhance the presentation? In what ways?

____ Did the presenter answer audience questions thoroughly and with clarity?

PRESENTATION

HOW TO TEACH PRESENTATION OF INFORMATION & IDEAS

GRADES K-2

	Description of the Step	Checklist for this Step
1	Teach how to understand the scope of the presentation: task, audience, purpose (refer to the "Decode a Prompt" tab)	____ What am I presenting? ____ To whom am I presenting? ____ Why am I presenting this information to this particular audience? ____ What materials do I need? ____ How many minutes do I have to present?
2	Teach students how to gather relevant information (refer to the "Forms of Media" tab)	____ Does my information come from text, video, or a speaker? ____ Have I taken notes from the text in my own words? ____ Did I clear up anything I was confused about by rereading? ____ Do I have information about each step or sequence of ideas that I am presenting? ____ Did I use other sources like the internet, another text, or ask an expert?
3	Teach students how to create recordings, drawings and multimedia to enhance their content (refer to the "Technology" tab)	____ Do I need to have visuals to help the audience understand the topic? ____ How will I visually share the topic and details with the audience? ____ How will I show my visual aid? ____ Should I add labels to my visual aid? ____ Will the audience be able to see the visual aid; is it big enough?
4	Teach students how to coherently outline their presentation and create opportunities for interaction with the audience	____ Have I created a way to introduce the topic to the audience? ____ Do I have notes or picture clues to help me remember the details I want to share in my presentation? ____ Do I have a way to make sure the audience is interested in my presentation? ____ Did I state information or recall details in my own words? ____ Have I practiced my presentation so I am not just reading my notes?
5	Teach students how to speak audibly, change their voice pattern/ volume for emphasis, repeat important points and make eye contact	____ Where do I need to use expression during my presentation? ____ What information or key points will I want to repeat to make a strong point? ____ What will I do if the audience looks like they are not interested in my topic? ____ How will I need to project my voice to make sure the audience can hear me?
6	Teach students how to ask relevant follow-up questions and provide feedback to the presenter	____ What can I ask the audience to do to show they understand the information I've presented? ____ How will the audience provide feedback to me about the presentation content and my presentation skills? ____ Will the audience be able to ask questions during and at the end of the presentation? ____ Does my presentation have a clear ending so the audience will know it is completed?

HOW TO TEACH PRESENTATION OF INFORMATION & IDEAS

GRADES 3-5

	Description of the Step	Checklist for this Step
1	Teach how to understand the scope of the presentation: task, audience, purpose (refer to the "Decode a Prompt" tab)	____ What topic am I presenting? ____ Who is the audience I am presenting to? ____ Why am I presenting this information to this particular audience? ____ Should I include my opinion or personal experiences with the topic? ____ Do I have enough time to share all that I've planned for?
2	Teach students how to gather relevant information (refer to the "Forms of Media" tab)	____ Did I use text to gather information about the topic? ____ Did I confirm information from other sources? ____ Do I have enough information about each step or sequence of events? ____ Have I considered another point of view? Should I share it? ____ Have I deleted unnecessary information?
3	Teach students how to create recordings, drawings and multimedia to enhance their content (refer to the "Technology" tab)	____ What kind of visual representation would convey the information most clearly? ____ Would adding an audio/video recording add to or take away from the presentation? ____ When should I use the audio or visual enhancement during my presentation for the biggest impact? ____ How big should my visuals be so they can be seen by the entire audience? Should I create a handout?
4	Teach students how to coherently outline their presentation and create opportunities for interaction with the audience	____ How will I introduce the topic to the audience? ____ Do I have notes to help me remember the details I want to share? ____ What engagement techniques will I use? ____ Did I state information or recall details in my own words? Do I need to use specific terms or vocabulary? ____ Are the content and the visual enhancements organized logically for a smooth presentation?
5	Teach students how to speak audibly, change their voice pattern/volume for emphasis, repeat important points and make eye contact	____ What attention grabber should I use to gain the audience's attention about the topic? ____ Have I practiced my presentation enough so I can make eye contact throughout? ____ Do I have sections in my presentation that require me to change my voice pattern/volume for emphasis?
6	Teach students how to ask relevant follow-up questions and provide feedback to the presenter	____ What question will I ask the audience to check for understanding? ____ What question will I ask the audience to see if the supporting details could be recalled? ____ How will I get feedback on how clearly I spoke? ____ Am I prepared for the audience to ask questions? ____ Am I able to lead the audience to other references for more information, if requested?

HOW TO TEACH PRESENTATION OF INFORMATION & IDEAS

GRADES 6-8

Description of the Step	Checklist for this Step
1 Teach how to understand the scope of the presentation: task, audience, purpose (refer to the "Decode a Prompt" tab)	____ What questions are we trying to answer in the presentation? ____ What role do I have in presenting the material? ____ What is my targeted audience? What is their bias? ____ What form of language should I use with the audience? Formal or informal? ____ How much time do I have to present?
2 Teach students how to gather relevant information (refer to the "Forms of Media" tab)	____ What information do I need in support of the topic? ____ What information do I need to counter a claim? ____ What information remains unclear or might require further questioning? ____ What sources should be included in the presentation? What will best help me highlight my point? ____ How much background information is needed for the audience?
3 Teach students how to create recordings, drawings and multimedia to enhance their content (refer to the "Technology" tab)	____ What information will be better presented visually? ____ What information can be enhanced by a chart or graph? ____ How might information be summarized on a slide? ____ What digital format or presentation system should I use for my presentation? ____ Is a recording available that could be added to the presentation?
4 Teach students how to coherently outline their presentation and create opportunities for interaction with the audience	____ Is the information organized in such a way to grab the audience's attention? ____ For each piece of evidence presented, is source material noted? ____ Are points made in order of importance? Am I stressing the main point repeatedly? ____ Where could I engage the audience by asking if they agree or disagree with information presented? ____ Is there any information that competes with or distracts from the content that needs to be removed?
5 Teach students how to speak audibly, change their voice pattern/volume for emphasis, repeat important points and make eye contact	____ Where in the presentation can I raise or lower my voice to create suspense or add interest? ____ Who in the audience can I make eye contact with while making a main point? ____ What is the appropriate tone to use for this presentation or audience? ____ Are the words chosen for my presentation appropriate for the audience? Does it take into account their potential bias and their background knowledge?
6 Teach students how to ask relevant follow-up questions and provide feedback to the presenter	Notes for the audience: ____ Is there a point in the presentation that lacked clarity? ____ Do you believe the speaker answered the question he meant to during the presentation and how do you know? ____ Do you have concerns about the information that was presented? What are they? ____ What further questions resulted from the presentation? ____ What could the speaker have done better?

HOW TO TEACH PRESENTATION OF INFORMATION & IDEAS

GRADES 9-12

	Description of the Step	Checklist for this Step
1	Teach how to understand the scope of the presentation: task, audience, purpose (refer to the "Decode a Prompt" tab)	_____ From what perspective should I deliver the presentation? _____ How might I best influence the audience during the presentation? _____ Am I familiar with vocabulary necessary to reach this audience? What are specific terms they know that I should use? _____ Can I present what I need to given the allotted time?
2	Teach students how to gather relevant information (refer to the "Forms of Media" tab)	_____ Does our library have source materials available to use on the topic? _____ Is computer-based research needed to further investigate the topic? _____ Have I included all claims and counter claims related to the topic? _____ Have I evaluated all my sources for credibility, accuracy and quality? _____ What source material is inconclusive or irrelevant and should not be used in my presentation?
3	Teach students how to create recordings, drawings and multimedia to enhance their content (refer to the "Technology" tab)	_____ Given my sources, what media should be used? _____ Do I have both qualitative and quantitative data to use in the presentation? _____ What is the best way to present that data – visually, mixed media or oral? _____ What is the best way to integrate media? What effect do I want it to have? _____ Are original recordings or videos available to use in my presentation?
4	Teach students how to coherently outline their presentation and create opportunities for interaction with the audience	_____ Are claims and counter claims organized in a way that make sense? _____ Have I considered the subject, occasion, audience and purpose? _____ Are rhetorical strategies or devices used to further understanding on the topic? _____ Does anything presented lead to any evidence that would be considered flawed?
5	Teach students how to speak audibly, change their voice pattern/volume for emphasis, repeat important points and make eye contact	_____ Are there points within the presentation where eye contact and voice projection will help emphasize my points? _____ Is my presentation appropriate in tone for the subject and the audience? _____ Is my language appropriate for the audience? _____ Are the claim, stance, and point of view appropriate for the audience? _____ How will I engage my audience? Note-taking? Questions? Engagement techniques?
6	Teach students how to ask relevant follow-up questions and provide feedback to the presenter	Notes for the audience: _____ Was there a point in the presentation that was exaggerated or inaccurate? _____ Did evidence presented advance the speaker's claims? How? _____ What additional questions resulted from the presentation? _____ What phrasing or words used by the speaker were most effective in conveying his stance? _____ How might further questions be answered? What additional evidence is needed?

HOW TO TEACH NOTE-TAKING

Note-taking is the practice of writing down the most important information from a piece of text, speaker, multimedia presentation or other source.

	DESCRIPTION OF EACH STEP
STEP 1	Teach students how to set up their notes: • date • format • columns • colored ink • page numbers
STEP 2	Teach students how to determine what constitutes important information versus trivial information
STEP 3	Teach students the clues that a speaker or writer gives when he is sharing important information
STEP 4	Teach students how to abbreviate consistently
STEP 5	Teach students when and how to quickly sketch graphs, charts and visuals during note-taking
STEP 6	Teach students to leave a blank space or line in their notes to denote missing information or something to follow-up on at a later time
STEP 7	Teach students to put question marks in their notes to indicate where they need to do further research or gather more information
STEP 8	Teach students how to annotate, pull out the most important terms and write a very brief summary statement from their notes

HOW TO TEACH NOTE-TAKING

CLUES THAT A SPEAKER GIVES THAT HE IS SHARING IMPORTANT INFORMATION

CLUES

COMMON ABBREVIATIONS

• Reviews main points in the introduction	
• Writes information on a chart, whiteboard or screen	
• Repeats ideas or phrases	
• Emphasizes points by changing voice and gestures	
• Emphasizes points by spending more time and giving more examples	
• Gives word signals (e.g. *"There are **two points of view** on...", "The **third** reason is...", "In **conclusion**..."*)	
• Provides lists of items	
• Summarizes points at the end	

b/c	because
b/4	before
cp.	compare
def.	definition
diff.	different, difference
ea.	each
e.g.	for example
fr.	from
etc.	and the rest, and so on
impt.	important
nec.	necessary
no.	number
pt.	point
p.	page (pp. = pages)
re.	regarding, about

HOW TO TEACH NOTE-TAKING

GRADES K-5

	Steps	Sample Script
1	Teach students how to set up their notes: date, format, columns, colored ink, page numbers	We're going to learn how to take notes about the important things we read and hear about. Notes help us organize and remember the most important information. We're going to keep our notes in the same manner so that each time we take notes we can focus our attention on what we are learning. Each of you has a sheet of paper. At the top of the paper you will write the title of the text or topic you're hearing/reading about. For example, today we're reading a text titled "All About Snakes." Watch me model for you where to write the title (write the title on the top line). Now, write that on the top of your paper. Now, notice that the paper is pre-folded and has a line drawn down the length. This is to help us organize the notes.
2	Teach how to determine what constitutes important information versus trivial information	Now, we need to decide what should be written in our notes. We want to include the most important things. So, for example, if we are reading about snakes and the author shares facts about snakes, we would jot down on the left-hand side of the page "facts." Any facts about snakes would be written underneath. Let's say that the author states that there are as many types of snakes as there are types of butterflies. We would not jot that down because our notes are on facts about snakes, not butterflies. While other information we read may be interesting, we are only taking notes on the most important information that we need to remember. Notice that I just wrote the main ideas down in a few words; I didn't write a complete sentence. **All About Snakes** **Facts** • Fast • Eat whole mice • Shed skin monthly
3	Teach clues that the speaker gives about note-worthy information	Authors organize their writing to get their most important points directly to the reader. Often, there are signal words like "first, next, last." In our text today, we see that there are other clue words, such as "there are three reasons for...." In the text we just read I noticed several clues and signal words that the author used. Here are several examples that I found: **All About Snakes** **Facts** • Fast — First... • Eat whole mice — Then... • Shed skin monthly — Next...

HOW TO TEACH NOTE-TAKING

GRADES K-5

	Steps	Sample Script
4	Teach students how to abbreviate consistently	*The notes we take need to be in our own words and as brief as possible. We need to find ways to help us become very efficient, which means the notes need to be complete, but we don't want to spend too much time rewriting whole pieces of text and sentences. So, we can use some abbreviations to help write in a quicker manner.* (Refer to the "Note-taking" tab for common abbreviations)
5	Teach students when and how to quickly sketch graphs, charts and visuals during note-taking	*Not only do we write words in our notes, but we can also add quick sketches to help us to organize and remember what we are learning.* *The key to adding sketches is to do them quickly...in seconds!* *For example, in our text about snakes the author wrote about the process of digestion. We can draw a graphic that shows the cycle like the one in the text. Watch me as I do that now.* **All About Snakes** **Facts** • Fast · First... • Eat whole mice · Then... • Shed skin monthly · Next...
6	Teach students how to leave blanks or spaces to fill in later	*Sometimes when we're listening to text or a speaker, the information can become overwhelming and we miss an important point or two. When this happens we can write down what we remember and leave a blank line for parts we missed. Then, we can ask the speaker for clarification or go back to the text and fill in the missing information.* *Watch me model that for you now.*
7	Teach students to put question marks in their notes to indicate what they need to gather more information about or clarify	*To show that we have questions about what we're reading or hearing, we can add a question mark next to our notes. This will remind us that we need to gather more information or clarify something that was confusing. I'm going to show you what that looks like in the third paragraph of our snakes selection. Watch me now.* **All About Snakes** **Facts** • Fast · First... • Eat whole mice · Then... • Shed skin monthly · Next... • _____ ? _____
8	Teach students how to annotate their notes so they pull out the most important terms	Model the following for students: • Show an annotated text and explain the annotations in the margins • Write the numbers next to the text where there are steps or sequential information • Circle the main idea and underline key words in the details that support the main idea

HOW TO TEACH NOTE-TAKING

GRADES 6-12

Steps	Sample Script
1 Teach students how to set up their notes: date, format, columns, colored ink, page numbers	*Today I'm going to teach you how to take notes on multiple texts that you read, presentations that you hear, or media clips that you see. At this level, it is important to be able to work with more than one central idea or topic in a single text, as well as be able to work with multiple pieces of texts about the same topic.* *When you take notes, you will use the same steps again and again in order to become proficient with note-taking.* *We are going to use the two texts we are currently reading,* ___(text 1)___ *and* ___(text 2)___ . *I need you to get set up for note-taking by taking out paper, a pencil, two colors of pens and the two texts we are using. Determine which color pen you will be using to take notes for text #1 and which color pen you will be using to taking notes for text #2.* ***Step One:*** *Please write the title of the two texts we are using on the top of your paper using the appropriate colored pen.* ***Step Two:*** *Using your pencil, we are going to draw a line down the page slightly to the left of the center. We want the left side for note-taking smaller than the right side. I will explain why later.* <table><tr><td>**Text 1 Title**</td><td>**Text 2 Title**</td></tr><tr><td></td><td></td></tr></table>
2 Teach how to determine what constitutes important information versus trivial information	*We will need to consolidate the information we have from these texts into manageable chunks. Remember to use the correct color so that you can keep track of which text you are referring to in your notes. This will play an important role as we might need to head into the text later to grab information we missed.* ***Step One:*** *Identify the main idea or topic of both texts.* *We have already determined that both of these texts cover the same topic. Be sure to write this on the left-hand side of your notes in one color pen and then underline it in the second color pen. This will indicate that the two texts cover the same central idea or topic. Watch me as I show you.* ***Step Two:*** *Identify key details from both texts.* *When we read the introduction in both texts, we can identify the key details supporting the central idea. On the right-hand column of the note sheet, write the key details supporting the central idea from text #1 in one color and from text #2 in a second color. If text #2 has key details that are the same as what you wrote down for text #1, then underline the key detail in the color for text #2 instead of re-writing the same key detail twice. Be sure to stick to the details that support the main idea, not the other information presented. Watch me as I show you.* <table><tr><td>**Text 1 Title**</td><td>**Text 2 Title**</td></tr><tr><td>Main/central ideas:</td><td>Key details:</td></tr></table>

HOW TO TEACH NOTE-TAKING

GRADES 6-12

Steps	Sample Script
3 Teach clues that the speaker gives about note-worthy information	*Now we are going to identify clues from both texts. Authors, presenters, and media narrators use clues to help organize their writing. These clue words and phrases are used to help the reader understand the material presented.* *On the left-hand column of our note sheet we will write down key vocabulary related to the main/central idea from text #1 and text #2 in their appropriate colors. Watch me as I show you.* <table><tr><td>**Text 1 Title**</td><td>**Text 2 Title**</td></tr><tr><td>Main/central ideas: Clue words:</td><td>Key details:</td></tr></table>
4 Teach students how to abbreviate consistently	*Remember common abbreviations used such as 1st = first, 2nd = second, w = with, w/o = without, & = and can be used to speed up our note-taking. Let's aim to use at least three abbreviations regularly as we take notes on the text from this point forward.* (Refer to the "Note-taking" tab for common abbreviations)
5 Teach students when and how to quickly sketch graphs, charts and visuals during note-taking	*There are some authors, presenters and media narrators that use visual effects in their writing or presentations. Sketching a picture is often useful to explain what we mean without using words.* *As we take notes, we need to ask ourselves "Is it easier/quicker to draw a sketch or to write the words to describe it in our notes?" Watch me as I show what I would draw.*
6 Teach students how to leave blanks or spaces to fill in later	*When we are taking notes, sometimes the presenter or media narrator moves through the material faster than we can jot it down.* *Don't forget to place an underline or leave a space for key pieces of information you missed.* *There are ways to gather this missing information after the speaker has finished. You may ask a speaker to repeat whatever point you missed or you may ask a fellow classmate if they could share the information with you.*
7 Teach students to put question marks in their notes to indicate what they need to gather more information about or clarify	*Many of the things we will read this year will require further investigation. As we take notes, we want to be sure to mark the points in our notes where the information is unclear, needs additional evidence, or causes us to ask further questions about a topic.* *For example, if I have a question about the evidence given for key detail number one. Over on the side of my notes, I will place a question mark (?) and a quick note "check source" or "need more info." This will help direct my research on the topic later.*
8 Teach students how to annotate their notes so they pull out the most important terms	*Remember that when I give you a copy of text, poem, story, etc., you may annotate directly on the paper. You can also go back through the notes you have taken and annotate your own notes by:* • *Underlining key words* • *Use a question mark where something is unclear* • *Use an exclamation point to note something that took you by surprise* • *Use numbers to identify steps or sequence of events*

HOW TO DECODE A PROMPT

When you **decode a prompt**, you read it closely to figure out what you are required to produce, who you are writing it for and why you are writing the piece.

TASK	AUDIENCE	PURPOSE
What am I writing?	For whom am I writing?	Why am I writing?

GUIDING QUESTIONS

Teach Students How to Figure Out the Task	• Is there important language in the prompt that gives me clues about what kind of writing I should do? • Should the language from the prompt be included in my writing? • Are there unknown terms in the prompt that I need to figure out? • Are there bullet points/call-out boxes in the prompt that give me clues or directions? • What type of writing should I produce? • What will it look like when I've finished?
Teach Students How to Figure Out the Audience	• What do I want the reader to know by the end of the text? • Does the reader have experience with or bias for/against this topic? • Does communicating with the reader require me to use technical, formal language? What clues tell me this? • Does communicating with the reader allow me to write informally? What clues tell me this?
Teach Students How to Figure Out the Purpose	• What am I writing in response to? What clues tell me this? • Am I writing to inform, persuade or entertain? • Am I writing to demonstrate my knowledge on this topic, as well? • Am I analyzing a topic or situation for the reader? • What strategy will I use to write this? • Is the topic broad or specific?

How to Teach Students to Critically Think About Text

HOW TO DECODE A PROMPT

AN EXAMPLE OF HOW TO DECODE A PROMPT

"The following is a rough draft of a paragraph that a student is writing for the school newspaper about why there should be a longer school day. The draft needs more details to support the **student's reasons** for having a longer school day.

Revise the paragraph by adding details from the daily schedule that help support the reasons for having a longer school day."

Task
What am I writing?

"The following is a rough draft of a paragraph that a student is writing for the school newspaper about **why** there should be a longer school day. The draft needs more details to **support the student's reasons** for having a longer school day.

Revise the paragraph by adding details from the **daily schedule** that help support the reasons for having a longer school day."

Purpose
Why am I writing?

Opinion Paragraph

"The following is a rough draft of a paragraph that a student is writing for the **school newspaper** about why there should be a longer school day. The draft needs more details to support the student's reasons for having a longer school day.

Revise the paragraph by adding details from the daily schedule that help support the reasons for having a longer school day."

Audience
For whom am I writing?

The students, staff, parents, school board and community members are readers of the newspaper

How to Teach Students to Critically Think About Text

HOW TO DECODE A PROMPT

GRADES K-2: SAMPLE ASSESSMENT PROMPTS BY TYPE

Selected Response

Sample

After reading the story, *A Dinosaur is the Best Pet*, choose the best answer for the following question.

Why is a dinosaur the best kind of pet?

A. Dinosaurs are fun to play with.
B. Dinosaurs make big messes.
C. Dinosaurs sleep all of the time.
D. Dinosaurs get you in trouble.

Read the following sentence from the _____ paragraph:

"_____."

The author uses the word _____ to show that:

A.
B.
C.
D.

Which sentence supports the idea that _____?

A.
B.
C.
D.

Constructed Response

Sample

In this passage, Miguel wants to travel the world. He has a list of places he wants to visit. How did this list change from the beginning of the story to the end of the story? Complete the sentence below.

Miguel wanted to visit _____ at the beginning of the story, but at the end of the story he wanted to visit _____ .

How did _____ change from the beginning of the story to the end of the story?

Support your answer by including _____ details from the story in your answer.

Write your answer in complete sentences.

Describe the challenge that the character _____ faces in the story, _____ , and how he responds.

Use _____ details from the text to support your answer.

Extended Response

Sample

In the story, Max learns how to write while he is at school. What have you learned to do in school? Write your answer in a complete sentence.

Read the sentences below from paragraph _____ of the story and answer the question that follows.

Compare and contrast how _____ in the story feels about _____ and how you might feel if you were in a similar situation.

Use complete sentences and details from the story in your response.

Both passages are about _____ .

What is the same about the _____ in the passages?

Write your answer in a complete sentence.

Technology Enhanced

Sample

Drag the sentences into correct order to show the beginning, middle, and end of the story, *A Dinosaur is the Best Pet*.

The dog chewed up Ruth's shoes, tore a pillow, and dumped the trash can.

The big plush stuffed dinosaur was a great pet that did not cause problems.

Ruth's mom said she could get a pet.

Read the sentences below from paragraph _____ of the story.

Click on the picture that shows where the story takes place.

Arrange the events from the passage in the order in which they happened by clicking on the sentences and dragging them into the correct order.

HOW TO DECODE A PROMPT

GRADES 3-5: SAMPLE ASSESSMENT QUESTIONS BY TYPE

Selected Response

Sample

Read the following sentence from the first paragraph:

"The waves shimmered like diamonds."

The author uses the word "diamonds" to show that:

A.   The girl was wishing for jewelry.
B.   The water looked sparkly.
C.   Diamonds were in the water.
D.   The water cost a lot.

A student is writing an informational report about _____. The student needs to edit information that does not support the topic sentence. Which sentence does not support the topic sentence and could be removed? A. Sentence 1 B. Sentence 2 C. Sentence 3 D. Sentence 4	Which term best describes how the information in the passage is organized? A. Cause and effect B. Order of importance C. Problem and solution D. Compare and contrast

Constructed Response

Sample

Closely reread the 2nd paragraph of the passage. How does this paragraph support the author's opinion about the quality of school lunches?

Write your answer in complete sentences.

A student is writing an informational paragraph about _____ for a class report. The paragraph needs an introduction. Read the paragraph and directions that follow. Write at least one sentence that could be added to the beginning of the paragraph to introduce the topic. Type your answer in the space provided.	The article tells about _____. Use two details from the text in your one sentence summary.

Extended Response

Sample

After reading the passage from *Animal Tracks & Signs* by Jinny Johnson, explain why animals build burrows and nests. Describe three examples of these animal homes. Use information from the passage to support your answer and write in complete sentences.

Based on the two passages, answer the following questions about _____. 1. Using the information from the text, why _____ ? 2. How is the information in _____ different from the book, _____ ? Use complete sentences to respond and cite at least three details from the text.	What does the author want the reader to learn from this passage: " _____ ,"? Use complete sentences in your answer and cite at least three details from the text.

Technology Enhanced

Sample

Read the passage found below. Highlight the topic sentence and underline the unnecessary information included in the passage.

The text describes the steps for _____. Arrange the sentences in chronological order. ☐ ☐ ☐ ☐ ☐	Based on the passage, highlight two questions that the reader should be able to completely answer after reading the text. A. _____ ? B. _____ ? C. _____ ? D. _____ ?

HOW TO DECODE A PROMPT

GRADES 6-8: SAMPLE ASSESSMENT QUESTIONS BY TYPE

Selected Response

Sample

Karen wants to revise the underlined sentence in her second paragraph. Which statement represents the best revision of the underlined sentence?

A. When people combine these foods with exercise, they stay healthy and energized.

B. These foods, when they are combined with exercise, can keep people healthy and energized.

C. These foods, when people are combining them with exercise, can keep people healthy and energized.

D. When these foods are combined by people with exercise, they can keep people healthy and energized.

The passage suggests all of the ideas about _____ except for:	Read the following paragraph from lines "_____" to "_____."
A.	Why does the author write "_____?"
B.	
C.	A.
D.	B.
	C.
	D.

Extended Response

Sample

Use information from the passage to write an argument about which school year model you think is best: the traditional model or the year-round model.

In the two passages that you read, _____ and _____, what central theme do they share? Write a paragraph outlining the similarities and differences in the authors' approaches to sharing the theme.	In a paragraph, describe how the two protagonists in _____ and _____ change over the course of both texts. Support your ideas with examples from the text.

Constructed Response

Sample

Write a concluding sentence for the passage about the way Annie John feels during her first morning at school. Support your answer with details from the passage.

Write a transitional sentence linking the scenes from _____ and _____.	Read the following sections of the text: _____. How do the phrases _____ and _____ reflect how the author feels about _____? Use two details from the text to support your answer.

Technology Enhanced

Sample

Read the statement below, and then answer the question that follows. "Joy Hakim, the author of this passage, admires Sojourner Truth for her ability to change peoples' ideas."

How can you tell that the above statement is true? Click on a sentence in the passage that could be used as evidence to support this statement.

From the list below, select two quotations that provide additional evidence to support _____. Drag and drop your answers into the boxes labeled "Evidence."	Determine the central idea in _____. Drag the best statement to the "Central Idea" box in the table. Then drag and drop into the table three supporting details to highlight how that idea is developed over the course of the text.

How to Construct a Performance Task

Performance Tasks are integrated, extended assessment tasks requiring students to use multiple skills/strategies simultaneously

1. What skills, strategies or standards am I assessing?
2. What context will the task be built around? (Theme, topic, text, current event or issue)
3. What stimulus will I provide? (Video, text, audio recording, visual)
4. What product will I expect? (Written, oral presentation, visual, media, combination of sources)
5. What task will they engage in? (Time, outside resources available, individual/group task, which items will be scored)
6. What constitutes a complete, thorough product?
7. What scoring template/rubric will I use?

HOW TO DECODE A PROMPT

GRADES 9-12: SAMPLE ASSESSMENT QUESTIONS BY TYPE

Selected Response

Sample

Madame Shaw seems to regard Polly more warmly than she does the other children. Click on the highlighted sentence from the story that provides the best evidence that Polly shares this feeling.

In this passage, "_____," the author uses figurative language to describe _____. Select the response that most closely matches the intended meaning. _____: A. B. C. D.	Read the following passage and then answer the question. Click on the sentence in the text that appears to be extraneous in relation to the main idea of the passage? A. B. C. D.

Constructed Response

Sample

In the passage, Dr. Mortimer speaks several times of a legend surrounding the Baskerville family. In one to two sentences, explain how the reader can tell that a frightening hound haunts the family. Support your answer using details from the text.

Read this sentence from the passage "_____." Explain how the author's use of _____, _____, and _____ suggest a bias. Type your answer in the space provided.	What does the author mean by _____? How is this information important as you analyze the outcome of _____. Use details from the text to support your answer.

Extended Response

Sample

Read *Daedalus and Icarus* by Ovid and *To a Friend Whose Work Has Come to Triumph* by Anne Sexton.

Use what you have learned from reading the texts to write an essay that provides a comparison of how Daedalus and Icarus are transformed in both pieces.

Explain how the author's choice to introduce _____ as he did, influenced your perception of _____. Provide evidence from the text to show how the author's choices shaped your understanding and viewpoint on _____.	In the space below, identify the sentences from the paragraph that are unnecessary, and briefly explain why each one should be removed.

Technology Enhanced

Sample

Below is the beginning of a student essay that needs to be edited for coherence and clarity. Read the paragraph. (Student reads *High School and Extracurricular Activities*)

Click on the underlined phrases in the passage and select from the drop down menu the most appropriate way to write each phrase to maintain the language and style of the paragraph.

Evaluate whether the evidence used in these paragraphs is relevant and comes from a credible source. Click on the highlighted statements and drag them to the appropriate boxes below.	Highlight the phrases within the text that best support the author's claim that _____.

How to Construct a Performance Task

Performance Tasks are integrated, extended assessment tasks requiring students to use multiple skills/strategies simultaneously

1. What skills, strategies or standards am I assessing?
2. What context will the task be built around? (Theme, topic, text, current event or issue)
3. What stimulus will I provide? (Video, text, audio recording, visual)
4. What product will I expect? (Written, oral presentation, visual, media, combination of sources)
5. What task will they engage in? (Time, outside resources available, individual/group task, which items will be scored)
6. What constitutes a complete, thorough product?
7. What scoring template/rubric will I use?

HOW TO ORGANIZE WRITING

Organized writing introduces a topic clearly, states an opinion or thought, and creates a coherent structure in which related ideas are grouped to support the writer's purpose and outcome.

FIVE STEPS TO ORGANIZED WRITING

STEP 1

Brain dump ideas

Jot down all of your ideas, without judgment or analysis

STEP 2

Cross out weak, unrelated or repetitious ideas

Get rid of ideas that just don't make sense, are not meaningfully connected to the others or are too similar to other ideas

STEP 3

Make connections between similar ideas

Draw lines between similar points and group ideas into logical categories

STEP 4

Order ideas

Number your categories by sequence, chronology or point of view

STEP 5

Start writing

HOW TO ORGANIZE WRITING

	DESCRIPTION
STEP 1 **Brain Dump**	Reasons why the school year should be shorter • So kids could get summer jobs for longer • So we get out before the summer heat comes • There is less time after testing to "let down" • We could learn up to the end of the year rather than tiring out quickly • Because May sounds like a better month to get out than June • We would have longer to recover over the summer and prepare for the Fall • Teachers wouldn't have to drag out topics over such a long time • It would allow for more family time • It would ease stress
STEP 2 **Cross Out**	• So kids could get summer jobs for longer • ~~So we get out before the summer heat comes~~ • ~~There is less time after testing to "let down"~~ • We could learn up to the end of the year rather than tiring out quickly • ~~Because May sounds like a better month to get out than June~~ • We would have longer to recover over the summer and prepare for the Fall • Teachers wouldn't have to drag out topics over such a long time • It would allow for more family time • It would ease stress
STEP 3 **Make Connections**	Free Time/Flexible Time • So kids could get summer jobs for longer • It would allow for more family time Decrease Stress/Better Learning • We could learn up to the end of the year rather than tiring out quickly • It would ease stress • We would have longer to recover over the summer and prepare for the Fall Teaching is Better • Teachers wouldn't have to drag out topics over such a long time
STEP 4 **Order Ideas**	First Idea: Decrease Stress/Better Learning • We could learn up to the end of the year rather than tiring out quickly • It would ease stress • We would have longer to recover over the summer and prepare for the Fall Second Idea: Teaching is Better • Teachers wouldn't have to drag out topics over such a long time Third Idea: Free Time/Flexible Time • So kids could get summer jobs for longer • It would allow for more family time
STEP 5 **Start Writing**	1. Introduction sentence 2. First idea from Step 4 + supporting statement 3. Linking statement 4. Second idea from Step 4 + supporting statement 5. Linking statement 6. Third idea from Step 4 + supporting statement 7. Restate first, second, and third points succinctly 8. Conclusion sentence

HOW TO ORGANIZE WRITING

GRADES K-2

Paragraph Form for Narrative Writing

I read the text, _____*(title of text)*_____. The main character in the story is _____*(main character)*_____. There are other characters too. Their names are _____*(other important characters)*_____. The story takes place at/in _____*(describe setting)*_____.

In the beginning of the story, the _____*(main character)*_____ _____*(action/event)*_____. As a result of that event, _____*(main character)*_____ _____*(actions of the main character)*_____. At the end of the story _____*(main character)*_____ _____*(actions or feelings of the main character*_____. The events of the story teach _____*(main character)*_____ a lesson. The lesson learned is _____*(central idea)*_____.

Refer to the "Summarize" tab for how to write a summary statement.

Paragraph Form for Informative Writing

I read the text, _____*(title of text)*_____ and it is mostly about _____*(topic of text)*_____. I learned interesting facts about _____*(topic)*_____ from the text. First, _____*(detail 1)*_____. Second, _____*(detail 2)*_____. Lastly, _____*(detail 3)*_____. In summary, the main topic of the text is _____*(summary)*_____.

Refer to the "Summarize" tab for how to write a summary statement.

HOW TO ORGANIZE WRITING

GRADES 3-5

✔ Paragraph Form for Narrative Writing

The story, _____(title of text)_____, begins with _____(describe setting)_____. The characters in the story are _____(list main characters)_____. At the beginning of the text _____(main character)_____ could be described as _____(description of main character)_____. By the end of the text _____(main character)_____ could be described as _____(description of the main character at the end of the story)_____. The change in _____(main character)_____ is a result of _____(reason[s] for the change in the main character, cite the details of the problem)_____. In summary, this story is mostly about _____(central idea)_____.

Refer to the "Summarize" tab for how to write a summary statement.

✔ Paragraph Form for Informative Writing

Reading _____(title of text)_____ allowed me to learn about _____(topic)_____. There was a lot of information shared by the author. _____(Author's name)_____ wrote that there are _____(number)_____ steps/stages in the process of _____(process)_____. The first step/stage is _____(step/stage 1)_____. (Add in one or two sentences to describe the first step/stage.) The second step/stage is _____(step/stage 2)_____. (Add in one or two sentences to describe the second step/stage). The next step/stage is _____(step/stage 3)_____. (Add in one or two sentences to describe the next step/stage). The final step/stage in _____(process)_____ is _____(last step/stage)_____. (Add in one or two sentences to describe the last step/stage). One thing I wonder/am confused about after reading the text is _____(state confusion or question related to the topic or details the author shared)_____. From the text I learned about _____(process)_____, which is important for _____(conclude why this process is important)_____.

Refer to the "Summarize" tab for how to write a summary statement.

HOW TO ORGANIZE WRITING

GRADES 6-8

✓ Paragraph Form for Narrative Writing

In the narrative, _____(title of text)_____, there are several significant details that help the reader follow the story. First, _____(detail telling who)_____. Another important detail is _____(detail telling what)_____. The third detail important to the story is _____(detail telling where)_____. Also significant is _____(detail telling when)_____. A key element of the story is _____(detail telling why)_____. Finally, the writer tells _____(detail telling how)_____. All of these details are significant because _____(conclusion)_____.

Refer to the "Summarize" tab for how to write a summary statement.

✓ Paragraph Form for Informative Writing

In the _____(title of text)_____, the problem/topic that arises is _____(problem/topic)_____. To find a solution to the problem, _____(author[s])_____ decides to _____(action 1)_____. After _____(action taken)_____, he tries to solve/resolve _____(problem)_____ by _____(action 2)_____. In order to solve/resolve the problem, he _____(action 3)_____. In the end, _____(action)_____ solved the problem by _____(evidence from text)_____.

Refer to the "Summarize" tab for how to write a summary statement.

HOW TO ORGANIZE WRITING

GRADES 9-12

✓ Paragraph Form for Narrative Writing

In the text, _____(title of text)_____, the author provides important information that characterizes _____(character)_____. First, we learn from _____(character)_____'s words and thoughts that _____(possible theme)_____. Evidence of this in the story is _____(evidence/detail 1)_____. Second, because of _____(character)_____'s actions, we learn that _____(possible theme)_____. An example of this is _____(evidence/detail 2)_____. Third, _____(character)_____ has an important goal, which is _____(character's goal)_____. An example of _____(character)_____'s real motivation is _____(motivation)_____. By the end of _____(title of text)_____, we learn a great deal about the character, _____(character)_____. We learn that he _____(conclusion and final theme)_____.

Refer to the "Summarize" tab for how to write a summary statement.

✓ Paragraph Form for Informative Writing

At the end of the text, _____(title of text)_____, I drew the conclusion that _____(concluding statement)_____. This conclusion is based on information in the _____(title of text)_____ and my personal knowledge. First, the author says/shows that _____(detail 1)_____. Second, _____(detail 2)_____. Another detail that leads up to the conclusion is _____(detail 3)_____. Personal experience and knowledge of the world also tells me that _____(personal knowledge detail 1, detail 2)_____. I can draw the conclusion that _____(conclusion)_____. Personal experience and general knowledge about _____(topic)_____ helped me to arrive at this conclusion.

Refer to the "Summarize" tab for how to write a summary statement.

HOW TO TEACH OPINION AND ARGUMENT

GRADES K-2: STEPS FOR WRITING AN OPINION PIECE

	Step	Definition	Clue Words	Discussion Starters
1	State your opinion about the topic	Opinion: a personal view about something	• My opinion is… • I believe that… • My personal view is…	• How do you feel about…? • Which is better…? • In your opinion what character is _____?
2	Identify and state three reasons for your opinion	Reason: an explanation	• One reason is… • Another reason for… • A final reason is…	• Why do you think…? • What are your reasons for…? • Using information from the text, what are _____ reasons to support your opinion?
3	Put your reasons in a logical sequence	Sequence: to put things in order	• The first reason is… • The main reason… • To begin with…	• What is the main reason…? • If you could only tell one reason for _____ what would it be? • After the main reason what would be the next reason for _____?
4	Write a concluding sentence	Concluding statement: a sentence that wraps up the paragraph and restates your opinion	• In conclusion… • As you can see… • For these reasons my opinion is…	• What is the topic and your opinion of the topic? • What key details should be restated in your conclusion? • Does the concluding statement provide a summary?

Opinion Frame

The text that I read was ___(title of text)___ . My favorite character is ___(favorite character)___ . One reason ___(favorite character)___ is my favorite is because ___(reason 1)___ . Another reason ___(favorite character)___ is my favorite is because ___(reason 2)___ . As you can see, ___(favorite character)___ is my favorite character.

Sample Opinion Paragraph

The text that I read was _Flora & Ulysses_ written by Kate DiCamillo. My favorite character is _Flora Belle_ . One reason _Flora Belle_ is my favorite is because _she likes to read comic books and so do I_ . Another reason _Flora Belle_ is my favorite is because _by the end of the story she has changed into a character that is optimistic_ . As you can see _Flora Belle_ is my favorite character.

HOW TO TEACH OPINION AND ARGUMENT

GRADES 3-5: STEPS FOR WRITING AN OPINION PIECE

	Step	Definition	Clue Words	Discussion Starters
1	State your opinion about the topic	Opinion: a personal view about something	• While I can understand some people feel _____, I feel _____. • Although the author's reasoning supports _____, I believe _____. • My opinion about _____ is the same as the author's in that... • My personal view is _____ even though the author states _____.	• What do you believe about _____? • Which is better/worse _____? • Based on what you've read and researched, what is your opinion?
2	Identify and state three reasons for your opinion	Reason: an explanation	• One reason is... • Another reason for... • A final reason is...	• Why do you think _____? • Why do you have that opinion? • If your opinion differs from the author's, what justification can you offer?
3	Put your reasons in a logical sequence	Sequence: a logical or purposeful order	• The first explanation is... • The main reason for my opinion is... • The primary reason is... • Another reason for my opinion is...	• If you could only tell one reason for _____ what would it be? • What is the primary explanation for your opinion? • After the main reason what would be the next reason for _____?
4	Write a concluding sentence	Concluding statement: a sentence that wraps up the paragraph and restates your opinion	• To sum it up... • Consequently... • Altogether...	• Does your conclusion summarize the reasons that support your opinion? • Does your conclusion encourage others to take action? • Does your conclusion convince the reader?

Opinion Frame

I think that _____ (topic) _____ is/are _____ (opinion) _____. **The first reason is** _____ (reason 1) _____. _(Write a sentence with details supporting reason 1)_ . **Another reason is** _____ (reason 2) _____. _(Write a sentence with details supporting reason 2)_ . **Finally, I think** _____ (topic) _____ is/are _____ (opinion) _____ **because** _____ (final reason) _____. _(Write a sentence with details supporting the final reason)_ . **In conclusion, I strongly believe** _____ (opinion) _____.

Sample Opinion Paragraph

I think that _using powdered milk in fry bread_ is _the best way to make traditional fry bread_ . **The first reason is** _the dough turns out lighter and fluffier_ . _Using regular milk makes the dough heavier and denser_ . **Another reason is** _keeping powdered milk available is easier_ . _The shelf life of powdered milk is much longer than regular, liquid milk_ . **Finally, I think** _powdered milk used for making fry bread is the best way to make traditional fry bread_ **because** _this is the way I saw it being made during a Pow Wow celebration_ . **In conclusion, I strongly believe** _that if you're trying to make light and tasty fry bread you should use powdered milk instead of regular liquid milk_ .

HOW TO TEACH OPINION AND ARGUMENT

GRADES 6-8: THE ANATOMY OF AN ARGUMENT

	Component	Definition	Clue Words	Discussion Starters
1	Claim	To state or assert that something is the case *Example: A lie detector test is not a valid measuring tool in an interrogation.*	• argument • position • supports • pro/con	• What is your claim and why? • Evaluate which are the most powerful or important claims. • How is your claim distinct from all others?
2	Evidence	Available facts or information indicating claim is true *Example: There is no evidence that any pattern of physiological reaction is unique to deception.*	• reasons • support data • to defend	• Did you locate and identify verifiable reasons/evidence that can be used to support the claims made? • How might you use data to support your claim? • How are reasons and evidence identified and used to support claims that defend a position?
3	Counterclaim	A claim made to counter a previous claim *Example: More often than not, lie detector test results corroborate the testimony in trials.*	• rebuttal • refute	• Which of these reasons/evidence can be proven true or false through research? • What evidence supports a pro position and what information supports a con position on an issue? • What are the key points *for* the issue and the key points *against* the issue?
4	Warrant	Explanation of why or how the data supports the claim, the underlying assumption that connects your data to your claim *Example: If it is indeed true that lie detector tests are not a valid tool during interrogations, then law enforcement agencies should not require people on trial to be subject to them.*	• justify • validate • sanction • conclude	• What is a convincing conclusion with a clincher or call to action? • Is a summary of reasons/evidence included?

HOW TO TEACH OPINION AND ARGUMENT

GRADES 9-12: THE ANATOMY OF AN ARGUMENT

	Component	Definition	Clue Words	Discussion Starters
1	Claim	State or assert that something is the case. Must be arguable and must require defense through evidence. *Example: There is not enough talk about where SNAP dollars actually go and whether the food stamps program is working.*	• argument • assertion • proposition • thesis	• What argument are you making about this topic or text? • How can you logically introduce your claim and support your reasoning? • How can this claim be effectively delivered to the audience or reader?
2	Evidence	Available facts or information indicating whether a belief or proposition is valid. *Example: A lax approach to purchases using food stamps, and a lack of transparency about where SNAP money is going, are threatening the program's true efficacy.*	• proof • confirmation • verification • corroboration • affirmation • substantiation	• Has evidence been gathered from multiple sources and does it include quotations, observations, interviews, examples, facts, data, results of surveys and/or experiments? • Has evidence been evaluated for quality and appropriateness for the topic? • How will you use your evidence to support your claim?
3	Counterclaim	A claim made to rebut a previous claim. *Example: While some object to proscribing the types of foods that can be purchased under SNAP as being paternalistic, such regulations are standard for other federal programs, such as school meals and WIC.*	• refutation • justification • countercharge • defense	• What evidence can be used to counter the claim made? • What alternate or counterclaims did you include? Are they fully developed? • Are your counterclaims precise, relevant and substantive?
4	Warrant	Explanation of why or how the data supports the claim, the underlying assumption that connects your data to your claim. *Example: We do not know how much money SNAP participants spend on Coke, for example, as opposed to milk; or Lucky Charms, as opposed to oatmeal. Despite the importance of such information in evaluating how well the program is meeting its stated nutrition goals, the federal government does not collect it.*	• closure • outcome • culmination • verification	• How do the ideas in the conclusion pull together the claim and evidence in a logical manner? • Does the conclusion help clarify and emphasize the relationships between claims, evidence and counterclaims? • Are additional questions generated from this conclusion to further research the topic?

HOW TO ANALYZE MEDIA

Analyzing forms of media is scrutinizing the source's author, the date it was written, the purpose of the piece and the intended audience.

Credible sources are articles, essays, journals, and other forms of text and communication that can be confidently quoted, referred to or cited. Credible sources are tested, accurate and professionally written.

✓

ONLINE SOURCE CREDIBILITY CHECKLIST FOR STUDENTS

- How did you find the site?

- What information is available about the author?

- Are there citations and dates?

- What is the domain name?

- Is the writing professional and obviously edited?

- Is the site well-designed and functional?

- Does it allow for unmonitored collaborative editing?

✓

QUESTIONS FOR ANALYZING SOCIAL MEDIA SOURCES

- Is the author close to the action or near the event as he reports?

- Who follows this person? Are followers commenting on posts or tweets and interacting with the author regularly?

- Are there other sources reporting the same information?

- Is this topic in line with other posts and tweets by the author? Can you gather more information on the topic by reading previous entries?

- How long ago was the account created? Does it have detailed information about the author? Does it include an actual picture of the author?

- Is the author referring to credible sources in his posts?

HOW TO ANALYZE MEDIA

	STEPS	DESCRIPTION OF EACH STEP
1	Teach students that there are three tiers of sources	**Tier 1:** Straight-from-the-source credible, first-hand or expert-level sources (most credible) **Tier 2:** Periodicals, journals, foundation newsletters and publications, and other authoritative, professionally edited sources (slightly less credible) **Tier 3:** Blogs, collaborative websites and unedited sources (least credible)
2	Once students understand the three tiers of sources, teach and model how to analyze forms of media by answering the question, "Who is the author and what do I know about him?"	__ Has the author cited sources? __ Is the author considered an expert in the field? __ Does the author have 'like' research or topics that he's written about or collaborated on?
3	Teach and model how to determine the date the source was written/ produced and whether it is relevant based upon that date	__ What time periods are relevant for this source? __ Does the source have to be current to be valid? __ Is the source routinely updated?
4	Teach and model how to figure out why the author produced the piece	__ What funding sources are fueling the writing? __ Is this a commercial piece or an informational piece? __ What other points of view/sources should I consider? __ How much does the author's affiliation or organization shape the message?
5	Teach and model what types of sources your students should value and count as credible	__ Do I require mainstream sources? __ Should I accept most internet sources without hesitation? __ Is the source written in a scholarly tone? __ Are peer-edited sources acceptable?
6	If using an internet source, teach and model this Step in addition to Steps 1-5	__ What is the domain name? (.edu, .gov, .mil and [state].us sites are likely to be more credible than .com, .org or .net sites) __ How did I find the site? Was it through a general search engine or through a trusted database? __ Are there advertisements throughout the site? __ Is the site generally well-designed and current?

HOW TO ANALYZE MEDIA

GRADES K-2

Step	Teacher Think Aloud
1	As I review ___(title of text)___ I can see that this text is a ___(Tier 1, 2, or 3)___ level and therefore is a ___(most, fairly, or least credible)___ source. I know this because ___(reason 1)___ and ___(reason 1)___.
2	We want to learn more about who the author is to help decide or determine if a source is credible and should be believed. As I read this text I want to ask myself if the author has cited or named his sources. I can see in ___(title of text)___ that ___(author)___ has/has not cited sources. (Show in the text where you found or would expect to find citations if none are cited). ___(Author)___ is thought of/not thought of as an expert in ___(field/topic)___. I know this because ___(author)___ has/has not written other works in the area of ___(topic)___.
3	The time period the source was written is important because information is constantly changing and may become outdated and unreliable. ___(Title of text)___ was written in ___(year)___. I find that by looking ___(show where you found the date of the source)___. The time period for ___(topic)___ is important/unimportant because ___(why it is important or unimportant regarding this topic)___.
4	When we consider the author's purpose for writing a text, this helps us to determine if the source is credible or not. ___(Title of text)___ was written for ___(purpose)___. If it was written for commercial purposes say: "Since ___(title of text)___ was written for commercial purposes, I know that it is supposed to encourage/discourage ___(paraphrase purpose)___. When I read sources that are written for commercial purposes, I have to ask myself what the other points of view are and should I/should I not be encouraged/discouraged to ___(topic)___." If it was written for informational purposes say: "___(Title of text)___ was written to inform me about ___(topic)___. It's important that I consider other points of view so I have all of the information instead of just this one source. I have to ask myself if the information I find in other sources is the same or different than in ___(title of text)___.
5	The person or group of people that would most likely read ___(title of text)___ would consider this source credible/not credible because ___(reasons to support claim)___.

HOW TO ANALYZE MEDIA

GRADES 3-5

Before I Read	• Did the author cite sources? Circle: Yes No
	
	    If yes, how many? _____(number of sources cited)_____
	
	• Is the author an expert on the topic of _____(topic)_____? Circle: Yes No
	
	    If yes, how do you know the author is an expert on the topic? _____(Write a sentence about how you know the author is an expert)_____ .
	
	• When was the text written? _____(date)_____
	
	• Is it necessary that the text was recently written in order to be considered credible? Why or why not?
	
	    Yes, it is important that the text was recently written, to be considered credible because _____(reason it's important that the text was recently written)_____ .
	
	    No, it is not important that the text was recently written, because _____(reason it's not important that the text was recently written)_____ .

While I Read	• What is the author's purpose for writing the text?
	
	    The _(author)_ **wrote** _(title of text)_ *for informational/commercial/entertainment purposes.*
	
	• What other points of view or sources of information should be considered?
	
	    A reader should consider _____(point of view or source)_____ *when reading about* _____(topic)_____ .

After I Read	• _____(Title of text)_____ should be considered a credible source because _____(three reasons source is credible)_____ . • _____(Title of text)_____ should not be considered a credible source because _____(three reasons source is not credible)_____ .

Sample Opinion Paragraph

• Did the author cite sources? Circle: (Yes) No

  If yes, how many? _____More than 5_____

• Is the author an expert on the topic of _____elephants_____? Circle: (Yes) No

  If yes, how do you know the author is an expert on the topic? _The front cover of the book tells us where the author has studied elephants. He lived in Africa and studied elephants for over twenty years._

• When was the text written? _____2008_____

• Is it necessary that the text was written recently to be considered credible? Why or why not?

  Yes it is important that the text _Eyewitness: Elephants_ was written recently to be considered credible because _the index of the book states part of the text will inform the reader about the impact of humans on the elephant population and habitat_ .

• What is the author's purpose for writing the text?

  Ian Redmond **wrote** _Eyewitness: Elephants_ for (informational)/ commercial purpose.

• What other points of view or sources of information should be considered about the topic?

  A reader should consider _the data from the dwindling elephant population_ *when reading about* _elephants_ .

  Eyewitness: Elephants should be considered a credible source because _it was written by a knowledgeable author, it is published work, and was written recently_ .

HOW TO ANALYZE MEDIA

GRADES 6-8

Think Aloud for Analyzing Forms of Media

In _(text and source)_ the author cited _(#)_ sources. The author of this text *is/is not* (underline choice) considered an expert in his field because _(three pieces of evidence that support the author being an expert)_ .

Continue with this sentence if the author is an expert: I know this because the author has researched similar topics of _(topic 1)_ , _(topic 2)_ , and _(topic 3)_ . *In addition, the author has collaborated on* _(other pieces author has written)_ .

Continue to next step if the author is not an expert: The _(source)_ *was produced in* _(date written)_ . *The date my source was written is/is not (underline choice) relevant to what I am currently researching because* _(reason for date being relevant or irrelevant)_ .

The author's purpose in writing this piece is _(commercial/informative/entertainment)_ . I know this because the funding source is _(example)_ . This piece of text is a commercial/informational (underline choice). My reasoning for this thinking is _(reason 1)_ . Other sources that I have considered in my research are _(sources)_ . I can justify that the author's view on this topic is biased/not biased (underline choice) because _(reason 1)_ , _(reason 2)_ , and _(reason 3)_ .

My audience for the research findings is/are _(classmates, teacher, expert, etc.)_ . _(Audience)_ *does/does not* (underline choice) require mainstream sources because _(reasons)_ . Peer edited sources are/are not (underline choice) acceptable by my audience.

The domain name of my source is _(source)_ . I found the site through _(search engine or database)_ . The overall design of the website is _(describe design and address advertisement use)_ .

Sample Opinion Paragraph

In Sea World's Earnings Disappoint Amid Animal-Rights Protests the author cited 6 sources. The author of this text is not considered an expert in his field.

The article was produced on August 13, 2014. The date my source was written Is relevant to what I am currently researching because my purpose for research is to prepare for a debate regarding current orca captivity.

The author's purpose in writing this piece is to inform his audience. This piece of text is informational. My reasoning for this thinking is that it's a newspaper called The Wall Street Journal. Other sources that I have considered in my research are PBS.org and Discovery.com. The author's message is that Sea World's earnings have gone down drastically. I can justify that the author's view on this topic is not biased because the author is a journalist for The Wall Street Journal.

The audience for my research findings is my classmates and teacher. My classmates and teacher do require mainstream sources because we are preparing for a debate in class. Peer edited sources are not acceptable by my audience.

The domain name of my source is .com. I found the site through Google. The overall design of the website is a newspaper that has categories, a search engine within the site, there are advertisements, and lots of links to other stories.

HOW TO ANALYZE MEDIA

GRADES 9-12

Checklist for Evaluating Sources

✓ **Check Publisher:** This media source was published or sponsored by _(publisher/sponsor)_ . This source is considered a credible source on the topic for the following reasons: _(describe why publisher is credible)_ .

✓ **Check Credentials:** The authors of this work are _(authors)_ . Their qualifications and degrees are _(qualification 1)_ , _(qualification 2)_ and _(qualification 3)_ . They are considered experts in the field of _(field of study)_ because _(reasons)_ .

✓ **Check Accuracy:** The statistics or facts about _(data or describe the facts)_ of this source are verified by other experts in the field. Cite additional experts and articles corroborating data or facts.

✓ **Check Dates:** The information in this source was published, _(date of publication)_ . Other information is available from _(source and publication date)_ . The source above provides the most current information on the topic.

✓ **Check Bias:** The authors, _(authors)_ , express the conflicting opinions of _(describe authors' opinions)_ . Author #1, _(author 1)_ , expresses a conflicting opinion from author #2, _(author 2)_ . These authors are biased in the following ways: _(quote from authors that expose bias and then explain why)_ . The data provided by _(author 1)_ and _(author 2)_ shows _(deficit in data provided and why that shows a bias)_ .

✓ **Check Audience:** These media sources are chosen because they are prepared for _(audience)_ . This audience is appropriate for this _(grade level or age)_ for which the information is being prepared.

✓ **Check Type of Source:** This source is a _(media type [for example: book, textbook, academic journal, trade journal, government report, legal document, press release, advertisement, flyer, pamphlet, radio or television broadcast, public meeting, web site, blog, message board, chat room, images, audio files])_ .

Signs That a Social Media Source Might be Outdated, Fake or Unreliable

- There is no interaction with fans or followers
- The source only "pushes out" content and does not engage
- The source "pushes out" links or spam messages repeatedly in a short amount of time
- The source shares misleading links
- There is no verification indicator on the profile
- The source is providing overly negative or positive reviews on products or services

HOW TO TEACH TECHNOLOGY

Technology is a digital tool for communicating, gathering and producing information.
Examples of digital tools that support literacy are: computers and their applications, software, internet searches, presentation programs, databases and web pages.

TOP 10 TECHNOLOGY SKILLS FOR K-2

1	Teach how to begin to operate a computer and other devices: turning the device on/off, logging in to/out of the device, using a mouse (clicking and dragging), and learning the main keyboard keys (letters, numbers, enter, shift, space bar, and delete/back)
2	Teach how to operate teacher designated websites and gaming tools to increase students' fluency with technology
3	Teach how to open, create, and save a word document
4	Teach how to copy and paste words and graphics into a word document
5	Teach how to type using two hands
6	Teach how to communicate ideas electronically, including text and graphics, in the form of presentations, electronic response tools, and simple graphing tools
7	Teach how to begin to understand what a database is and how to access stored materials
8	Teach how to safely use technology (e.g. what information to share or not share with others in a variety of situations, such as email, gaming and internet sites)
9	Teach how to browse the internet for information with the teacher's guidance
10	Teach how to determine the purpose for various media sources

TOP 10 TECHNOLOGY SKILLS FOR 3-5

1	Teach how to log in to personal accounts within school programs, assessments and educational programs, and web-based tool accounts
2	Teach how to select a printer and print features including design and layout settings, print preview, and page set-up
3	Teach how to use shortcut keyboarding skills for tasks such as copy/paste, undo and delete, in order to be more efficient with document creation and editing
4	Teach how to organize and locate files by understanding file paths
5	Teach how to type using two hands in order to meet the requirements of typing at least 25 WPM by the end of fifth grade
6	Teach how to create and edit presentations by taking and editing photos, then uploading and downloading the photos
7	Teach how to navigate internet browsers including the back, forward, favorites, and history tabs
8	Teach how to communicate and blog with other peers via a school based email system and safe internet tools
9	Teach how to search, use, and communicate with others safely on the internet, as well as how to configure privacy settings
10	Teach how to evaluate a website's accuracy and relevance

How to Teach Students to Critically Think About Text

HOW TO TEACH TECHNOLOGY

TOP 10 TECHNOLOGY SKILLS FOR 6-8

1	Teach how to create, save, open, import and use word processing (tabs, indents, headers, footers, endnotes, bullets and numbering, tables, etc.)
2	Teach copyright laws and guidelines and how to abide by them
3	Teach how to avoid plagiarism and copyright infringement by using fact-checking tools
4	Teach how to use various programs and communication tools (shared documents, discussion groups, web conferences, etc.) for communication, collaboration and productivity
5	Teach how to use effective search and browsing techniques using a variety of computing devices (probeware, handheld computers, digital cameras, scanners) to collect, analyze and present information
6	Teach how to use telecommunication tools (emails, discussion groups, web pages, blogs, web conferences, etc.) to collaborate and communicate with peers and others
7	Teach how to plan, design and develop a media project to present research and findings
8	Teach how to create a multimedia presentation using various media (audio, video, animations, etc.)
9	Teach how to use spreadsheets to organize and present data with simple charts and graphs
10	Teach how to perform simple operations (browse, sort, filter, search, delete data, enter data, etc.) in a database

TOP 10 TECHNOLOGY SKILLS FOR 9-12

1	Teach how to use word processing editing features (tracking changes, inserting comments, etc.)
2	Teach how to link multimedia products (e.g. word processing document to a spreadsheet)
3	Teach how to write citations for text and images from electronic sources
4	Teach terminology related to web authoring (HTML, URL, links, browsers, plug-ins, web servers, etc.)
5	Teach how to compare, evaluate and select appropriate electronic resources to locate information
6	Teach how to use communication tools (chats, instant messaging, blogs, wikis) both formally and informally
7	Teach how to implement a collaborative project with people in other locations using telecommunication tools (emails, discussion groups, web pages, blogs, web conferencing, etc.)
8	Teach how to use authoring tools (HTML, URL, links, etc.) to create multimedia products
9	Teach how to use various formatting options to convey information in charts and graphs (columns, templates, styles)
10	Teach how to use specialized technology tools (simulation software or computer-aided design) for problem-solving, decision making, and creativity across all subject areas

How to Teach Students to Critically Think About Text

HOW TO TEACH TECHNOLOGY

GRADES K-2

Month	Your Nine Month Plan for Teaching Technology Skills	
1	**Teach how to** turn on and off, log into/out of the device, use a mouse (clicking and dragging), and find/use the main keys (letters, numbers, enter, shift, space bar, and delete/back)	**Mastered Skills:** ____ Turn on/off a computer and other devices ____ Log in/out of a computer account set up by the school
2	**Teach how to** operate teacher designated websites and gaming tools to increase students' fluency with technology **Teach how to** open, create, and save a word processing document	**Mastered Skills:** ____ Use of a mouse (clicking and dragging) ____ Know the main keyboard keys (letters, numbers, enter, shift, and delete)
3	**Teach how to** copy and paste words and graphics into a word processing document **Teach how to** type using two hands	**Mastered Skills:** ____ Open, create, and save a word processing document ____ Copy and paste (words and graphics) into a word processing document
4	**Teach how to** communicate ideas such as text and graphics, in the form of presentations, electronic response tools, and simple graphing tools to share data	**Mastered Skills:** ____ Operate teacher designated websites and gaming tools
5	**Teach how to** understand what a database is and how to access stored materials	**Mastered Skills:** ____ Communicate ideas electronically, including text and graphics
6	**Teach how to** use technology safely, including which information to share or not share with others in a variety of situations (email, gaming, and internet sites)	**Mastered Skills:** ____ Understand what a database is and how to access stored materials
7	**Teach how to** browse the internet for information with teacher's choice of topic and sites	**Mastered Skills:** ____ Safely use technology
8	**Teach how to** determine the purpose for media messages as they appear in print and speech online (inform, persuade, commercial, entertain)	**Mastered Skills:** ____ Browse the internet for information with teacher's guidance of topic and sites ____ Determine the purpose for media messages as done with print, text and speech
9	**Firm up** skills from Months 1 to 8	**Mastered Skills:** ____ Use email to communicate with other students

HOW TO TEACH TECHNOLOGY

GRADES 3-5

Month	Your Nine Month Plan for Teaching Technology Skills	
1	**Teach how to** log into personal accounts within school programs, assessments, educational programs, and web-based tool accounts **Teach how to** select a printer and print features including design and layout setting, print preview and page set-up	**Mastered Skills:** ____ Log into personal accounts and web-based tool accounts
2	**Teach how to** use shortcut keyboarding skills for tasks such as copy/paste, undo, delete, and to move text during document creation and editing **Teach how to** organize and locate files and understand file paths	**Mastered Skills:** ____ Select a printer and print features including design and layout setting, print preview, and page set-up
3	**Teach how to** type using two hands (at least 25 WPM by end of fifth grade)	**Mastered Skills:** ____ Organize and locate files by file paths
4	**Teach how to** create and edit presentations, take and edit photos, and upload and download photos	**Mastered Skills:** ____ Use shortcut keyboarding skills for tasks such as copy/paste, undo, delete, and to move text during document creation and editing
5	**Teach how to** navigate internet browsers including back, forward, favorites tab, and history tab	**Mastered Skills:** ____ Create and edit presentations, take and edit photos, and upload and download photos
6	**Teach how to** communicate and blog with other peers via a school based email system and safe internet tools	**Mastered Skills:** ____ Navigate internet browsers including back, forward, favorites tab, and history tab
7	**Teach how to** safely search, use, and communicate with others on websites and gaming applications and understand the possible consequences of misuse **Teach how to** configure privacy settings	**Mastered Skills:** ____ Communicate and blog with other peers via a school based email system and safe internet tools
8	**Teach how to** consider the message's purpose and to evaluate the website's accuracy and relevance	**Mastered Skills:** ____ Safely search, use, and communicate with others on websites and gaming applications ____ Configure privacy settings
9	**Firm up** skills from Months 1 to 8	**Mastered Skills:** ____ Type using two hands at least 25 WPM by the end of fifth grade ____ Evaluate a website's accuracy and relevance

HOW TO TEACH TECHNOLOGY

GRADES 6-8

Month	Your Nine Month Plan for Teaching Technology Skills	
1	**Teach how to** use a variety of online technology tools (dictionary, thesaurus, grammar check, calculator) **Teach how to** create, save, open, import and use word processing documents (tabs, indents, headers, footers, endnotes, bullets & numbering, tables)	Mastered Skills begin month 2
2	**Teach how to** abide by copyright laws and guidelines **Teach how to** write non-plagiarized text by using online fact-checking tools	**Mastered Skills:** ____ Use a variety of online technology tools ____ Create, save, open, import and use word processing documents
3	**Teach how to** use technology (shared docs, discussion groups, web conferences) for communication, collaboration and productivity	**Mastered Skills:** ____ Abide by copyright laws ____ Avoid plagiarism by using online fact-checking tools
4	**Teach how to** use effective search and browsing techniques **Teach how to** use a variety of computing devices (probeware, handheld computers, digital cameras, scanners) to collect, analyze and present information	**Mastered Skills:** ____ Use technology for communication, collaboration and productivity
5	**Teach how to** use telecommunication tools (e-mails, discussion groups, web pages, blogs, web conferences) to collaborate and communicate with peers and others	**Mastered Skills:** ____ Use effective search and browsing techniques ____ Use a variety of devices to collect, analyze and present information
6	**Teach how to** plan, design and develop a media project to present research and findings	**Mastered Skills:** ____ Use telecommunication tools to collaborate and communicate
7	**Teach how to** create a multimedia presentation using various forms of media (audio, video, animations)	**Mastered Skills:** ____ Plan, design and develop a media project to present research and findings
8	**Teach how to** use spreadsheets to organize and present data with simple charts and graphs	**Mastered Skills:** ____ Create a multimedia presentation using various forms of media
9	**Teach how to** perform simple operations (browse, sort, filter, search, delete data, enter data) in a database	**Mastered Skills:** ____ Use spreadsheets to organize and present data with simple charts and graphs ____ Perform simple operations in a database

HOW TO TEACH TECHNOLOGY

GRADES 9-12

Month	Your Nine Month Plan for Teaching Technology Skills	
1	**Teach how to** use word processing editing features (tracking changes, insert comments) **Teach how to** link multimedia products (eg word processing document to a spreadsheet)	**Mastered Skills begin month 2**
2	**Teach how to** write citations for text and images from electronic sources	**Mastered Skills:** ____ Use word processing editing features ____ Link multimedia products
3	**Teach** terminology related to web authoring (HTML, URL, links, browsers, plug-ins, web servers)	**Mastered Skills:** ____ Write citations for text and images from electronic sources
4	**Teach how to** compare, evaluate and select appropriate electronic resources to locate information	**Mastered Skills:** ____ Use terminology related to web authoring
5	**Teach how to** use communication tools (chats, instant messaging, blogs, wikis)	**Mastered Skills:** ____ Compare, evaluate and select appropriate electronic resources to locate information
6	**Teach how to** complete a collaborative project with people in another location using telecommunication tools (emails, discussion groups, web pages, blogs, web conferencing)	**Mastered Skills:** ____ Use communication tools
7	**Teach how to** use authoring tools (HTML, URL, links) to create multimedia products	**Mastered Skills:** ____ Complete a collaborative project with people in another location using telecommunication tools
8	**Teach how to** use various formatting options to convey information in charts and graphs (columns, templates, styles)	**Mastered Skills:** ____ Use authoring tools to create multimedia products
9	**Teach how to** use specialized technology tools (simulation software or computer-aided design) for problem-solving, decision making, and creativity across subject areas	**Mastered Skills:** ____ Use various formatting options to convey information in charts and graphs ____ Begin to use specialized technology tools (simulation software or computer-aided design) for problem-solving, decision making, and creativity across subject areas